# FROM FEAR TO FREEDOM

## A Beautiful Anthology of Powerful Stories.

PUBLISHED BY: WOM ENTERPRISES

COPYRIGHT 2016
ALL RIGHTS RESERVED


NO PART OF THIS PUBLICATION MAY BE REPRODUCED, STORED INA RETRIEVAL SYSTEM, OR TRANSMITTED IN ANY FORM OR BY ANY MEANS, ELECTRONIC, MECHANICAL, PHOTOCOPY, RECORDING, OR ANY OTHER, WITHOUT THE PRIOR PERMISSION OF THE AUTHOR.

# Dedication

This book is dedicated first and foremost to God and His amazing grace and favor! I am so blessed to be able to follow my calling and to help other women to share their voices and change the world.

I want to mention the first person who told me I would change the world. It was Papa, George Henry Vandygriff. He stepped in and filled the role of Dad when my Dad chose to step out. I am forever grateful for him and my uncles for always being there for me. I know my Papa and Uncle Dennis are in heaven smiling down on me. And to my favorite Uncle Don "EX" Rogers, thank you for being my confident, my protector, my champion and keeper of my secrets!

I also want to thank all the women who trusted me with their stories, who believed in this project and chose to be brave and tell their testimony! Thank you and may God Bless you always.

*Now the Lord is the Spirit, and where the Spirit of the Lord is, there is freedom.*
*II Corinthians 2:17 (NIV)*

# Rev. Rhonda Branch Yearby

**Foreword Prayer**

Fear, it is the one thing that will keep us from experiencing freedom. Freedom. It is a life that we choose by letting go and letting God take control!

**I sought the LORD, and he answered me; he delivered me from all my fears. Psalm 34:4 (NIV)**

Heavenly Father, I thank you for healing the lives of those who are authors in *From Fear To Freedom* and those lives that will be changed by reading this book. I thank you for Teresa Hawley Howard and Women On A Mission Enterprises for inspiring so many lives! I thank you for your freedom. Your freedom that was paid for by the blood of your son Jesus Christ. Thank you for your guidance in our daily faith walk. Thank you that fear is decreasing and faith is increasing

Thank you for delivering those who read this book out of the bondage of fear. And that you are bringing them into a place of freedom because your word declares where your spirit is there is total freedom! Lord, I declare that the spirit of fear would no longer remain in lives of your people and that you would set them free by the power of your anointing.
In Jesus name, Amen.

# TABLE OF CONTENTS

Dedication .................................................................... 3

Rev. Rhonda Branch Yearby ........................................ 4

Teresa Hawley-Howard ............................................... 7

Skylee Mae Collins ..................................................... 10

Charmaine E. Betty-Singleton .................................... 12

Clara Peters ................................................................ 19

Donya Zimmerman ..................................................... 24

OLEVIA H HALL .......................................................... 30

Sherri Wade ............................................................... 36

Fred & Ingrid Edwards ................................................ 41

Elizabeth Blade .......................................................... 46

Duwanda S. Epps ....................................................... 49

Raffine' LaJuan .......................................................... 55

Nakia P. Evans ........................................................... 60

Aneisha Rush LeMonier .............................................. 65

Teresa Sisson ............................................................. 74

Angela Thomas Smith ................................................ 79

Placida Acheru ........................................................... 87

Deborah Stevens ........................................................ 94

Katrina M. Walker .................................................... 100

Tina Garner .............................................................. 105

Phyllis Turner ........................................................... 109

Shirley La Tour ......................................................... 116

Dormeka Pearce ....................................................... 125

Karen Tants .............................................................. 130

Vicki Cruz ............................................................. 138

Sheree Wright ....................................................... 145

Lisannia E. McIntyre ........................................... 158

Teri S. King .......................................................... 166

Sharon Gulley ...................................................... 173

Joy S. Pedersen .................................................... 180

Robyn Vintiner .................................................... 188

OLGA GONZALEZ ............................................. 195

Addie Lamour ...................................................... 202

Anu Mari Holopainen ......................................... 210

Francia Noble ....................................................... 219

Winnie Smith ....................................................... 226

Cami Ferry ............................................................ 236

Dr Dikabo Mogopodi ........................................... 242

Charmella Y. Smith ............................................. 248

Christine DiDio ................................................... 254

Conclusion ............................................................ 262

# Teresa Hawley-Howard

**From Fear to My Destiny**

There will come a time in your life when someone close to you will betray you. When your world will come down around your ears. You will see no way out. The darkness will be everywhere.

It is in these moments our faith is tested. These moments will define you, set the pace, show your merit, and your faith. Will you run? Will you cower? Will you lash out? Will you strike back?

Or will you turn to God, to His Word, and His Guidance? Will you hit your knees and allow God to use your situation? God will use your pain, your anguish, what the devil meant to destroy you. Will you allow God to raise you from the pit? Let him take you places you never dreamed.

He took Joseph from his pit of betrayal to the Palace! From the evil plan to God's glorious plan! Joseph had no idea of God's plan for him. He was faithful and obedient. No matter what his circumstances looked like, he trusted God.

### "Joseph said to them, "Do not be afraid, for am I in the place of God? BUT AS FOR YOU, <u>YOU MEANT EVIL AGAINST ME; BUT GOD MEANT IT FOR GOOD</u>, IN ORDER TO BRING IT ABOUT AS IT IS THIS DAY, TO SAVE MANY PEOPLE ALIVE" Genesis 50:19-20

He will open doors you never even knew existed. Doors you never planned to walk through. He will use you to lead others to Christ.

I faced this recently and honestly; I was unsure of my answer. I was afraid and sure it would be the end of my dream, my business and my future. I was paralyzed by that fear. And I was afraid and unsure of my next move. So did the only thing I knew to do in my time of darkness and uncertainty.

I cried out to God. He answered me! He led and protected me. He already knew the betrayal was coming. He had prepared my path. I am a child of God! My future is in his hands. He is the master of my destiny. And I will willing follow his lead. Without fear or hesitation. Knowing that Freedom is what he has planned for me!

The freedom he has for me is greater than I ever imagined! His plans so much grander and magnificent than mine. His vision for my life and my business so much more than my own. I only had to believe and have faith. To trust in the Lord and lean on him. Find my refuge and my strength in Him. And know He was preparing me for greater victories.

His will not mine be done! I will serve with a glad and cheery heart. I will follow where he leads me.

So, from my fear… Came my destiny! Time for you to find yours!

Teresa Hawley-Howard is a domestic violence survivor and an advocate. Her mission in life is to help other women find their voice and share their stories! She also wants to help them walk through their pain, limitations, and their own doubt to live the life they deserve. She knows their words, stories, scars, and their pain can inspire, heal and give hope to another woman. She is an empowerment/writing coach, speaker, #1 international best-selling author, radio host, and CASA volunteer. She is also Co-Founder of Tribute Magazine, spotlighting women. Founder of Women on A Mission, inspiring and uplifting women to live the life they desire. Radio Host of WOM Radio show, and host of Modern Day Woman Podcast! Teresa's goal is to help 10k women share their stories! Reach out and let Teresa help you share your story!

She is also the founder of Women on a Mission Enterprises. WOM Enterprises offers complete publishing packages for authors! The company offers several ways to become an author! You can write in one of many anthologies or you can write your own book! Either way you will become a published author! Share your story, promote your business and create your legacy! WOM Enterprises will help you make your dream become a reality. So stop procrastinating and become an author today with Women on a Mission Enterprises.

# Skylee Mae Collins

Original Poetry

Our Father in Heaven
Who watches over us daily
And loves us always.


F—fantastic

R—real

E—even for me

E—even for you

D—dreams

O—our father's plan

M—magnificent

**God loves everyone
He loves me
He loves you
Will you love him?**

Skylee Mae Collins is a fifth grader. She is ten years old. She is a big sister to Tommy Wayne and LillyAnne! And an author of her own book. She wants to take care of animals and write her stories. She is amazing and super smart! Her love shows in everything she does.

# Charmaine E. Betty-Singleton

*Where the spirit of the Lord is there is liberty.*
*2 Corinthians 3 o17 (NJV)*

*The Lord is close to the broken hearted and save those who are crushed in spirit. Psalm 34 o 18 (NJV)*

One may ask, "How does one escape from fear?" The simple but liberating answer is being obedient to God. Specifically, fearing God heading His word leads to having an abundant life versus fearing the unknown and succumbing to the little voice inside your head that causes you to be doubtful and live in fear. When you have the spirit of the Lord with you it causes you to obey the Lord and no matter the situation or obstacle you can face and not be afraid of it or the outcome.

To make this very plain I have learned over time to fear God like I feared my parents. My parents, now deceased, were my everything, I tried my best as a child not to do anything to disrespect my parents or bring shame or disgrace to the family name. That fear followed me throughout my childhood and remains with me to this day. I realized that people in my neighborhood were watching me and if I failed to obey my parents and did something wrong, they would report my inappropriate actions to my parents and I would get in trouble. To be honest as a child I was mad that the "so-called" neighborhood watch snitched on me and I walked around in an unhealthy state of fear that kept in bondage (in my mind) because I was afraid of getting a whipping. But once I realized if I just did what I was told to do, be where I was supposed to be and say what I was supposed to say life for the most part would be great. I took the spirit of my parents with me which caused me to conform my behavior to my parents' standards. And as a result, the more obedient I was the more responsibility and privileges I was given. Why? Because I could be trusted. I no longer worried about my neighbors in the community talking to my parents or trying to go blocks out my way for my "nosy" neighbors not to see me playing or talking to friends because I tried to be on my best behavior even when no one was looking and knew the report to my parents even though perceived to be bad would still work out for my good.

Let me tell you two quick stories about perceived bad reports. The first concerns a boyfriend of mine when I was about 17 years old. I was a short and petite teenager and my boyfriend at the time was very tall and well built. An older well concerned neighbor reported to my parents that I was hanging out with a boy, who was considerable older than me. My parents got a kick out of this because they met and had interrogated my boyfriend before I was allowed to date him and knew he was only one year older than me. The second story concerns me buying a dress for my mother's high school reunion (I was going to attend this event with her).

I went to one of the neighborhood stores which my mom and I frequently went too, however, on this occasion I went by myself. I found the dress that I wanted asked the owner to put it aside for me and told him I would come back in two days to purchase it when I got paid. He said he would in a very pleasant manner (his usual self, the same demeanor when my mom purchased items from him), I left the store and went home. A couple hours later, my mom came home laughing. She informed me that the store owner had stopped her as she was walking by as if he was waiting on her, and proceeded to show her the dress I picked out telling her that the dress was a little bit "too grown" for me. My mom then explained to him that I was 23 years old, at home for the summer from law school and working at a legal publishing firm. He apologized and kept saying that I looked so young. These people had my best interest at heart and out of respect for my family wanted to ensure my safety and reputation. I can now truly can say I appreciate their concern but more important I appreciate the relationship I had with my parents. Because I had surrendered to my parents' ways and submitted to their instructions I could walk around my neighborhood knowing all was well and my parents had my back. That's freedom knowing that they fought my battles and I did not have too.

This same concept applies to our relationship with God our Father. When we surrender all to God and submit to His instructions we obtain more responsibility more privileges and He has our back. He fights our battles if we allow him too. This requires obedience. I realized as a Christian I was not obedient to God. I must admit I am very independent I like to be in control, and I love to analyze and fix problems. Just give me a task; and I will complete it. I'm good at what I do. I am a subject matter expert. Thus, unconsciously I only half obeyed God because He would give me something to do and I either did my work, at my time or did not ask for guidance or clarification. Thus, I messed up a lot and I lived in fear of my past actions and mistakes. Because I failed to obey God I did not have his spirit with me and I was in bondage not only was I afraid of my past I feared the future because there were several things I did not want anyone to know about. While all looked well on the outside I was a mess on the inside and living in bondage.

And although God sees and knows all...my "neighborhood" was/is Jesus and the Holy Ghost. However, they did not tell on me, rather they interceded on my behalf as God rendered His punishment. God allowed certain things to happen to demonstrate to me than He (not I) is in control. That I needed to listen and obey Him. That I had to diligently seek His face in all things and allow God to order my steps, even when it did not make sense. As I learned to obey, which is not easy, I started to heal and was able to face my past/mistakes. I now am able to talk about my failures as God has transformed my mess into messages to help others. At the appropriate time He leads me to share my testimony about failed relationships, divorce, depression, low self-esteem, loneliness, failed business transactions and identity theft to the right individual or group. I'm no longer afraid of what others may think or say about me because God has my back and He fights my battles. All perceived negative reports about me are actually good and God my Father and I can laugh about them. I walk with my head held high knowing that as long as I am in obedience no weapon formed against me shall prosper, that I am fearfully and wonderfully made, that I can count it all joy because the joy of the Lord is my strength. Whom shall I fear? This so liberating. Glory to our God!!!!!

Also once I submitted all to Him, God clearly showed me that one of my biggest faults was being scared to ask others for help. Because I had been hurt on more than one occasion I did not trust others to help me with anything. Therefore, I did a lot of things myself, relying on me. Additionally, I failed to listen to God when he ordered me to ask others for help. I would pray ask and you shall receive and God would tell to go ask a specific person for help and I would tell God no, I'm asking you as my Father no one else. You are too providing not them. Because of fear I missed out on several blessings. I was in bondage to those past hurts.

However, God our Father is so faithful and wants the best for us. So although I stubbornly refused to listen, He eventually put me in a situation where I had to obey and follow His instructions. As I stated previously, I was constantly praying to God ask and you shall receive and when I did He showed me a person I needed to go to ask for help. The strange thing is that person told me if I needed anything to ask for it because if I didn't he was afraid that when I did he would not have anything to give. When he said that I said no everything is okay God will provide.  Well I was praying for a financial blessing to participate in major event in Jamaica WI everything was okay until there was a mix up with the fee for the hotel room.  Anyway I needed additional funding not only for myself but also for my roommate since she paid me through PayPal and I did not have access to the funds. God knew that because I was responsible for someone else's accommodations I would eventually ask for help. And I did. Imagine this I left home not having paid for the hotel reservation got on a plane and on my layover God said call and ask for help.

After some delay, I begrudgingly got on the phone and called my friend (who I did not know that well) and asked to borrow some money.  He immediately said okay let me discuss it with my wife (doubt tried to set in) and I said ok I'll wait for your phone call. Five minutes later, he called back asked for my account number and wired me the funds. By the time I landed in Jamaica I had more than enough money to pay for the hotel reservations.  Two weeks later I was blessed with enough money to pay him back with interest because God told me to do so. I later found out that because both he and I were obedient to God that money is still blessing others because when I paid him back he invested that money into his ministry to assist others in need.  Look how our God works, our obedience to God not only freed me but also freed others. I'm shouting as I write this because God loved me so much that he took the time to create an opportunity that would free me from my fear of asking for help.

And now because He trusts me in this area, He has created more opportunities that has resulted in blessings.  For example, one night I was talking to a friend on the phone and after the conversation ended God said to me pay Him first.  I said God I don't owe him any money. God said pay him.  He gave me an amount and I donated that amount to the person ministry. Seven days later I was at a speaking engagement and they had asked how much did I charge and I replied whatever you collect as a love offering is fine. I received the same amount I had donated to my friend.

Another, example of God's faithfulness and that I know He has my back if I only listen Him is that he told me to go Vegas, attend a certain conference and I would receive a blessing. I step out on faith and did what God instructed and went to Vegas. I arrived Friday night and the conference was to start Saturday morning. Well about 1030pm I received a call that the conference was cancelled. I was disappointed and was questioning God. That Saturday I met with one of the conference coordinators and received my blessing. I had been looking for an artist to draw pictures for a book I was writing (I had already asked several people with no success) and the coordinator was able to assist me. Look how God works if you just obey him.

I could go on and on providing more examples. My life is so different now that I make an honest effort to take the spirit of the Lord with me in everything that I do and obey God even when it hurts to do so or doesn't make any sense. By seeking God, obeying his instructions and activating my faith, relationships with others are so much better, I am happy when I go to work and other events, my health and sleep pattern has improved because I am not stressed out anymore, and I can honestly say that no matter what happens I count it all joy. I am free to be me. I do not live in fear; I live in freedom. Recently, God has told be to ask for what I think is almost impossible to receive. He told me just trusts Him. And because I do trust Him and I am not afraid of receiving a negative response I going to do what God has told me to do. He has not failed me yet.

Obey his word and be emancipated. Boldly obtain your destiny and live in freedom knowing that God has your back.

> For I know the plans I have for you," declares the LORD, "plans to prosper you and not to harm you, plans to give you hope and a future. Jeremiah 29:11 (NIV)

Charmaine E. Betty-Singleton, author, advocate, veteran, entrepreneur, attorney, and motivational speaker extraordinaire, is the CEO/Owner of PTK Enterprises LLC, a business focused on supporting other business owners, community activism, and empowering individuals to greatness. Additionally, she is the owner of Victorious Vibes radio station housed on SIBN. Charmaine is an avid lover of God and all people. She attributes her success first to God, and then to her parents and mentors, one of which is the late Dr. Myles Munroe. Charmaine strongly believes that with God ALL things are possible and wishes to "die empty" successfully fulfilling ALL that God has called her to do. Charmaine is a native of Kingston, Jamaica and refers to Queens, New York as home.

PTK Enterprises LLC, Ph: 850-550-6053; Website: www.ptkenterprisesllc.com
Twitter: ptkenterprisesllc@ptkenterprises;
Facebook: http://www.facebook.com/pages/PTK-Enterprises-LLC/344088438980115?ref=hl

Instagram: https://www.instagram.com/ptkenterprisesllc/

# Clara Peters

**Finding my Freedom**

When you have been trapped in a world of fear it becomes hard. Once your freedom arrives you have to trust and believe that he heard your cry and you must at least try.

Here I am on this journey of saying yes to being me for the first time in life! Not having the fear of what life will be when he comes home or when I get there. Those days came from me just not thinking negative and just saying this is the day. What I meant by that exactly, not sure, but I would assume that it is; that I will have a day of no negative.

God showed me that I'm going to release that thing from you. I need you to walk in your freedom with peace joy and happiness. A person should never live in fear of the unknown because of past hurt. When he sends you into the unknown or unfamiliarity's because he's giving you what you desire the most. Freedom to live life the way you want and not have any worries if you can or will succeed.

As I came out of the relationship I had been in for over 20 years with my ex-husband. I had another fear and that was I was single for this first time in life with 2 children still at home to raise. I had the freedom I wanted from that abusive marriage yet I didn't want to be a failure to my children.

With God on my side I did it, it wasn't so bad once we got used to living with just the 3 of us and not the 5 of us. My oldest was grown at this time and with her own family. Life is about what you make it. What I set out to do was keep the communication alive with my kids and let them know they had a voice. I made me my priority and in that the fear disappeared. I started becoming in my own and loving the life I was dealt until fear set in again.

This time the fear came when I ended up in the hospital being told I have a heart condition. I went from one hospital at 9ish at night to another after 2 days. Then once there in the middle of the night, they moved me from my nice private room to ICU. That's really when the fear came. I didn't have my mother here to help me through this crisis. She was back home sick; fighting what we found out 2 1/2 weeks after my diagnosis that was cancer. Lord, how am I going to do this alone? How am I going to get what I wanted so bad, my freedom to live a life of peace joy happiness and love?

With my children and grandchildren, he showed me that I can beat anything. Because they were not going to leave me; they were going to be right there for me. Together we beat the heart condition that the doctors said I would have for the rest of my life. They were amazed. They didn't understand how I ended up with it in the first place. I was healthy in good shape for a woman my age, but God stepped in and said trust me so I did.

From 2004 - 2010 I fought for my healing and I won. New found freedom came. Yet through the process he showed me that I had to endure the things in life to be a VOICE for others that's walking in abuse or diagnosis from doctors. For those not believing that they can turn that thing around by just trusting in him. A person has to trust and believe in self and know that we can do all things through Christ as he gives us strength. We need the power to say yes I can and the courage to move beyond that which we thought we couldn't.

Once I realized that I could have a beautiful stress free life after abuse; I vowed that I was going to not let fear find me again. Yet it did but I had to talk that giant down and move on! I've been through too much to allow the heartache of life's craziness to take me back there.

What did I do to finally say yes to my freedom? I started loving me more dating me and getting to find out what it is that makes Clara happy. I know I have received more than I had hoped for, I had desired, I had even imagined or thought. It hasn't been all good but it has been worth it because I learned.

I'm grateful for the freedom he has allowed me to have in the midst of 3-year battle to being divorced to losing my Queen and the diagnosis from doctors. I lived life with many regrets but not anymore. My thing has been to Live Laugh Love with no REGRETS! When I'm older I don't want to be saying I wish I would have when knowing I could have! Fear is real and it stops people from living life to the fullest.

One of my missions in life has become to encourage people to live and stop just existing! And not allow the fear of their past to stop them from where God wants to take them. Share my testimony and let them know they too can have freedom! Just take the leap of faith and God will give them their joy, their love, their everything! You just need surrender to him!

Through my fear he birthed my ministry Women of Divine Distinction Ministry! This year I celebrates 7years. Seven is the year of completion. Going into the 8th year, which is new beginning and I believe there's a new that awaits me. He has not failed me and I will not him.

As he has given me the freedom to truly walk into my true authentic self and not allow the hell from my past to stop me. I strive each day to better myself. I set myself on a daily mission to live life to the fullest by enjoying me falling in love with me. Enjoying the life God gives me daily to ensure that don't forget that I am not in that cocoon anymore. Where I was controlled and where I was living according to others but I am free!

Each day as I draw new strength to face new distractions. I make sure that I keep a positive mindset as know that the enemy is trying hard to keep me from going higher in the season of elevation that he has me in. The enemy tries me through my health yet I don't give up, I won't give up as he brought me too far.

When he birthed my ministry Women of Divine Distinction Ministry he told me that **"I am a VOICE for the VOICELESS"**. That meant that I have to share my story of abuse. That no matter what; I didn't do anything other than allowed my abuser to repeatedly abuse me. I needed to not just forgive him but also to forgive myself.

Through my freedom he gives me the peace I need to move about my life. To be free to say yes to me and when I say NO I mean it now! Before I felt guilty and ended up changing my mind and did what I was told or asked. I always hated the deck of cards I was dealt but I had to remember that I can change the course. I am the lead actress in my life story and what happens since he set me free it was on me. He showed me that I can conqueror any and all things. I can be and do all things through him that gives me the strength to wake up, to keep moving, to speak, and to be just the authentic me.

I used to question him, I don't anymore. Jeremiah 5:1 tells me that he had already said! Where I would be and what I would be doing in this season in my life? It is truly blessing me to live out my purpose even though it came via pain. Yes, I had to endure pain in order to see my purpose in life. As I continue to walk in my purpose and destiny in my life; I continue to connect with that butterfly! He brought to my vision many days to show me that I was in that cocoon yet He took me from that season of being control. You will break free from that and you will be like that butterfly that was set free to fly freely! According to what God sees fit for your life my child. He showed me and He can show you too!


Clara Peters is a woman of God. She has several events coming up! Please reach out to her @
www.womenofdivinedistinction.com
Wodd.2011@yahoo.com

# Donya Zimmerman

### Disbarred: Making a Major Comeback

Imagine being told that you can no longer do what you love to do anymore. That happened to me on June 12, 2012, when I received the letter from the Maryland Attorney Grievance Commission stating that "I had been disbarred for mishandling clients' funds and failure to represent clients competently". Based on this information, you may judge me as a bad attorney or bad person. But, one thing I have learned is not to judge a book by its cover. You must read the words in the book to get the full picture and understanding of the entire story. I was taken back when I received the letter, but I was not surprised by the disbarment. It was a great relief to let go of my law practice. I had clocked out of being an effective lawyer in 2010 (two years earlier) because I was tired of the rat race of the legal profession. But, I did not have the resources or support needed to bow out gracefully. I was too concerned about letting people down and fitting in with others.

My success, as an attorney, was built on impressing others. Instead of worrying about self, I was worried about others. I allowed others to influence my decision making power when it came to my law practice. I was taking advice from individuals, who never owned a business, on how to run my law practice. I hired individuals I knew I could not afford to pay and who didn't have the experience I needed to help run my practice. I never knew how to say "No". This is one habit I am becoming very comfortable with now. I have no problem with saying "No", even if, I have had said "Yes". I have learned to put my needs into consideration when making decisions concerning my personal and professional life.

One major mistake I noticed entrepreneurs make is that they try to hire their family members to work for them. It is okay to hire an experienced individual to work for you who is not a family member. You must understand that sometimes family can be your worst enemy and they can hinder your growth. Being an entrepreneur or business owner is a lonely journey you must being willing to take. Be careful who you share your dreams, goals, and desires with because there are many "wolves in sheep clothing". Those "wolves in sheep clothing" are normally the people closest to you.

As a second time entrepreneur, I am creating a tribe of people who can assist me with taking my business, Powerful Biz Woman, to great heights. When, I was an attorney, I didn't have the support I have now. I was taught how to be an effective litigator, but not the business of running a law practice. Lawyers are never given the tools and resources needed to operate a thriving law practice. The legal field is setup as "every lawyer for themselves". I see a stark difference in the business consulting arena because collaboration is seen as a key component to having a successful business. I have never been surrounded by so many business owners who have no problem with working together to grow each other's business. As a lawyer, I did not have a "tribe of fellow business owners" to support me. I felt like a person stranded on an island without life support the last two years as an attorney.

I have no regrets of having to hit rock bottom and having to re-invent myself as a business owner. It took me from 2012 to now to find my niche and the courage to be willing to share my story of being disbarred as an attorney. I had to let go of the guilt and shame of being disbarred. I had to let go of the "phony" friends who left once I lost my law practice. I had to allow God to strip me clean from the mess of my law practice to be able to move forward with starting my new business.

I took my legal skills and crafted them in a way that I could start all over again with a new business and new attitude. I became the "comeback kid" who had a story to share with others who have suffered a major setback and do not know that they can have a major comeback waiting for them. God reminded me on a daily basis that I had everything I needed to start over and live an abundant life. I had to get out of my own damn way to become the "Powerful Biz Woman" God destined me to become.

I was in the wilderness for about four years (2012 to 2016) because I had to be purged and cleansed of all the toxic packages I was holding onto from losing my law practice, my home, my finances, and lose of so called friends. Once I was purged of the toxic packages, I was able to receive what God had for me to become a successful entrepreneur. I had to learn that I should not compare my story to the story of others. Everyone has their own special story to share. We all have unique stories that can help someone.

I have learned to use discernment when it comes to making major decisions concerning my business. I have learned that every opportunity may not be beneficial to my personal and professional growth. I have learned that some rejections turn into awesome opportunities. Recently, I was turned down to become a certified teacher, but then God reminded me that I received free training and would not have to pay the $6,000 for it. Also, God reminded me that I should not be distracted from my ultimate goal of becoming a successful speaker, author, and trainer. I have learned not to sweat the minor setbacks and to adjust my plans to move forward.

Being disbarred reminded me of the importance of being humble and remembering that you can't achieve much without God. God is the reason I am living and the reason I am still standing after losing my law license. Without God I would not have made it through the rough patches of losing my law practice. When I went through the wilderness, I had to move back in with my Grandmother. I didn't see it as a blessing of being able to return home; I saw it as an embarrassment. Others may not have someone to return home to when needed. It took me four years to realize how blessed I was to have family there when I needed them. Don't be afraid to ask for help and reach out to others because you can't make it alone.

I had to stop acting like nothing was wrong and I had to stop being embarrassed of losing my law practice. I had to realize that I did something that people were afraid to do; and that was starting my own business. I started my own law practice at the age of 28 years old and I had a successful business for about 15 years. God reminded me of what I had accomplished as a young black female. I was not born to work a 9 to 5 job; I was born to create jobs for others. I was born to help others create their own jobs as business owners. God created me for greatness and not mediocrity. You are created for greatness and not mediocrity. Stop settling for the ordinary and expect extraordinary for your life.

I am still learning how not to just settle and be complacent. I am learning to push myself; and I am looking beyond my current circumstances. It took me about four years to finally sit down and write my story of being disbarred. It took me meeting Lori Pelzer and having a deep conversation about sharing my story with the world. I am blessed that Teresa Hawley Howard invited me to be a part of this wonderful collaboration of sharing my story.

I was afraid to share my story of being disbarred, but I realized that I was allowing my story to own me. This story was controlling how I lived my life and I was not using the story to make my life better. I was keeping my story to myself and not sharing it with the world. My story can be used by someone to inspire them to get moving on making their dreams a reality. My story can encourage someone to move forward and no longer allow their setback to hold them back. It is time to turn your "mess" into a "message" to share with the world. Your "message" can improve someone's life. We all have a story to share and it is time to write it down. Once you write it down, it is time share it with others because your story can be an inspiration to someone.

In closing, "Disbarred: Making a Major Comeback" has been therapy for me because I am releasing the hurt and pain. I am now allowing healing to come into my life and my past no longer controls my life. I am no longer carrying the baggage of being a disbarred attorney. I am a business consultant, author, trainer, and entrepreneur who has a message to share with the world. Time to let go of the baggage and set yourself up for your major comeback. I am gearing up for my major comeback. I pray this story encourages you to turn your "mess" into a "message" to share with an individual who needs it. Your message will help someone with moving forward with their major comeback. To God be the glory.

Donya Zimmerman is the principle owner of Powerful Biz Woman (DBA of FACMBC). She is a business consultant, author, and public speaker/trainer. Donya received her Juris Doctorate (JD) in Law from University of Baltimore Law School. Donya has a segment entitled "Powerful Biz Tip of the Week" on the Radio Show "Revolutionary Woman Radio" hosted by Khadija Ali that runs every Monday at 5:30 pm. Donya is a contributing writer with the Maryland Daily Examiner Newspaper and Leadership Girl Newsletter. She is a contributing writer with Rejoicing Hope online magazine. Donya has made article contributions to the Simply Inspirational Women in Business Journal for 2014 & 2015 published by Dr. Cheryl Cottle. She has her own blog site entitled "Business Development and Conflict Resolution" discussing business development, conflict resolution, and the daily life of being a small business owner. She has a business training series "Why CYA (Cover Your Assets) Letters Are Important for Business" that educates individuals on how to protect their business and personal assets while in business. Donya has also conducted several workshops and speaking engagements on business startups and female entrepreneurship. Donya has a few books in the pipeline that will be published in the latter part of 2016. The books titles are: 1. Daily Devotionals for Entrepreneurs & 2. How to Create a Strong Inner Will Power.

Donya has a strong desire to educate business owners on the importance of protecting their personal assets from legal and financial issues that may come up while in business. Donya has had to overcome major hurdles as a second time business owner. Donya at one time had a thriving law practice, but had to close her law practice due to legal and financial issues. Donya shares her story to ensure that other business owners and entrepreneurs do not face the same pitfalls that will cause them to have to close their business doors.

If you would like to contact Donya Zimmerman for business consulting services or to speak at your next engagement, here is her contact information:

Donya Zimmerman
Powerful Biz Woman
443-635-4557
dzimmerman36@gmail.com
https://www.facebook.com/FACMBC
https://www.facebook.com/PowerfulBizWoman
http://dzimmerman36.wordpress.com
https://twitter.com/FACMBC

# OLEVIA H HALL

### MY LIFE HAD NO VALUE TO ME

You always ask yourself, what is life and what does it mean? We hear people all the time say no one values life anymore. I can say that is true for the most part about myself, see I didn't care. A long time ago I was reckless with my life. I hated myself; I was so consumed with grief, depression and hurt that my life wasn't important. I was abused by so many people and I all I did was drink to dull the pain and sleep with random men. That was my life in a bottle and in a bed. No, that wasn't how I planned it but that was what I was living. I drank to ease the pain and I slept around because I felt unloved. When we go through something tragic and don't learn how to cope we give it an outlet in a negative way.

I was sleeping with men for money; meeting them at different places. I went to one home and it freaked me out it was dark and he never turned a light on as we proceeded to have sex; his niceness turned dark and all of sudden he was choking me and saying all kinds of crazy things to me I was praying I didn't die in his home. When it was over; I hurried to my car and left I was so scared but yet I didn't stop. I would continue to meet men.

I even placed ads on the internet and made up fake names to speak with them. After the last encounter, I decided that I would meet them at motels or hotels. I thought it was safer; the devil had me. I had Allowed all of the past hurt to control me. I honored the liquor. My kids weren't as important as I thought. Because I was steady doing risky and crazy things with my life. When we submit to the devil and allow him to have free reign over our life; at that moment, we have made him our God. I didn't believe that God was real. Yeah, I had gotten out some situations and yeah, I mean God helped me or so I thought. I was messed up for real and I didn't think that I deserve to be loved by God. I was a prostitute and a drunk. Speaking it out loud sounds so nasty. But that is what I was; I had sold myself for money.

In Genesis 1:26-27, it says we are made in His image, the very image of God. I don't think my image was good. I hated what I saw in the mirror. So I avoided the mirrors. My sins were so ugly to me. I couldn't take looking at myself. I would hear little things being spoken to me.

Psalm 139:13-16 says we are fearfully and wonderfully made. Who me? Impossible! I was a woman that was raped, beaten, homeless with her kids and had married two men that didn't love me but abused me.

My life wasn't right. I would get up and pretend all was okay. I would go to church, act and smile as if everything was good in my life. It wasn't! I was dying on the inside bleeding and no one knew! No one could help! I was scared! My kids were needing things. I was in between jobs.

I really couldn't hold a job; my drinking was so bad. I was spending the money I had to pay bills to go get drunk. While making my kids suffer with me, but I said I loved them. I remember, I decided I wanted a relationship so I met a guy on line and he was nice. I was really into him; he would come from Lake Charles to see me. Eventually spend the weekend with me and the kids. That seemed so normal! Until I realized, he was living a lie. He was pretending to be single and all the while having a wife.

My drinking had slowed down. I wasn't meeting random men. I thought, I had met the perfect guy. No such thing; it was fake. And how did I deal? I ended and started back to my old ways self-destruction.

I couldn't lead by example. I wasn't a role model to my kids especially my girls. I was living a lie. So I went back down my dark path. I felt deep down it was something I was supposed to be doing in my life. God always spoke to me while I slept and it was always clear. What I was to do. I had given up on my life; the drinking, the men, and the overeating all of that had a root cause.

Until I faced the mirror, the devil was going to kill me. It wasn't until I went home for a wedding; that I realized I had to do something about my weight. It wasn't until I realized that the female I was hanging with wasn't really a friend. How could I call her that? If she did try to stop me from engaging in reckless activities and knowing I was meeting men on line and sleeping with them. Drinking and driving drunk all the time, but yet said nothing. I really couldn't hold her at fault because I was grown and my choices were my own, at what point did I stop?

There came a moment that I was tired of everything. I just wanted to die and make all the pain go away. So I had to do what I didn't want to do and that was pray. I was tired of being the way I was, tired of hurting tired of being used and I just needed all of the emptiness to go away.

The devil was still at me though telling me I didn't need to talk to God. I wanted freedom in my life, so I lived on the edge and I wanted thrill and excitement.

I had to call on the Lord! I had to get on my knees and pray to Jesus to help me!

**1 Corinthians 15:34 Awake to righteousness, and sin not; for some have not the knowledge of God. I speak this to your shame.**

I had to pray and listen to what God was telling me! He asked was my life of any value to me? Did my kids mean anything to me? Did the fact he had spared my life more than once, but not once, not twice but more than three occasions. How could I take it all for granted? I had a purpose and he had given me an assignment, that I had to fulfill. I cried out to him "SAVE ME"!

He did and when I awaken the next morning I instantly told myself I was not drinking anymore! The temptation came that same female; called and invited me to come drink. I told her no! She was shocked and paused; she said just one drink! I said no again! At that moment who she was; God revealed because she said I hate you b**ch! I wasn't surprised! God had showed me that she would turn on me.

The next thing he revealed was not to call everyone a friend. As it turns out a guy we both knew had come on to me. but because I knew they had slept together; I refused his advances and told him that he had slept with my friend he laughed and said that's what you call her, huh. He then went on to tell me how she had been telling him all kinds of things about me. Some true; some lies. It showed me that I couldn't trust her. After he finished I simply thanked him and went into prayer. God will show you. He will give you discernment! we close our eyes and choose to be blind by the things we that He shows us. I never told her what he said I distanced myself from her.

I went through withdrawal from the drinking! I was shaking and crying but I refused to let the devil win. I defeated him because as June 1st 2016 I will have been sober for 2 years! All praises to God.

I deactivated the accounts I took the numbers out of my phone. If you take stuff out of sight; it is out of mind! I learned to value myself more! I learned to love myself! I learned that God is in me. When I realized that Greater is he that is in me than that is in the world! No weapon formed against me Shall prosper.

I was taught that sleeping with all those men and letting them have their way was not of God. He tells us that our body is not of our own! I had to respect God and myself better! So cutting them off and praying over myself was hard because I was always tempted! when things seem to get hard for me; I turned to the bible.

### 1 Corinthians 6: 19-20

**Or do you not know that your body is a temple of the Holy Spirit within you, whom you have from God? You are not your own, for you were bought with a price. So glorify God in your body.**

The blood is what saved me! It was the blood of Jesus that gave my life value! It was by his stripes that I am able to live and walk in God's love. And by Him alone; so when I become tempted or scared I lean not onto my understanding. I lean onto God's word. Knowing that because he died and arose for our sins that is why I should value my life! God gave his only son for me and my sins so I now live by his word and encourage others that fear is not an option when we have God.

We have to learn to love ourselves even in the storms and in the darkest moments of our lives! We have to know that God is with us at all times. In the beginning, I asked "What was my life worth?" Now, I can say it is Worth everything to me. I now realize, all we have to do is call on his name!

**"I Love Me", "I Value My Life", I live as if each day might be my last but I know I am free in Jesus.**

Olevia Henderson Hall was born and raised for the most part of her life in Shreveport, Louisiana. She currently resides in Houston, TX. She is the mother of 7, five daughters and two sons and the grandmother of four.

She recently became a self-published so she adds Author to her bio. She is also a Motivational Speaker and Life Coach & Advocate for Domestic Violence & Sexual Assault Victims. Olevia is Founder of Rebuilt Ministry where her mission is to bring others into the Kingdom under God's teaching.

She is the owner of her own business; Texas Legal Ease where she provides a multi services. God placed a calling in her life to open **(R.A.E) ** Rebuilding After Escaping the new Safe Haven Home opening in fall of 2017. She is a Woman of God who loves giving back who loves encouraging and empowering others as she is a survivor of abuse on all levels yet she is glad her faith in God never wavered.

Olevia is now married to her soulmate William Hall Jr and happy and living under God's commands. Olevia is Founder and Director of an Anti – Bullying Foundation known as HABB (Healing After Being Bullied) Olevia lives to spread God's word and help others.

# Sherri Wade

**FROM FEAR TO FREEDOM!**

This was inspired in part by my own experiences and from the works of Peter Phalam, Wayne Dyer, and Doreen Virtue.

I was raised in a fear based environment. A friend told me FEAR is an acronym for False Evidence Appearing Real. Fear has enslaved more minds and souls than slavery ever did. Many of us, myself included were raised to be "God fearing people." I am living proof that a person despite their circumstances can grow *From Fear to Freedom*.

I learned from personal experience that writing is cathartic, but Doreen Virtue taught me when others read about trauma, it can be devastating and negatively impact the reader. Your brain cannot always distinguish between a real life experience and an experience only read or heard about. It is because of this knowledge that I will not share my personal trauma and emotional pain.

I cannot imagine what it must have been like for a mom in her early twenties having three small children to support on her own. My dad passed away at an early age. When you grow up in a single-parent household wondering where the next meal is going to come from, worried about money, shelter, things. Children should never have to worry about such things that force you to learn fear at an early age.

"The fear of the Lord is the beginning of wisdom." Proverbs 9:10. Taken literally, some might think it means God is right around the corner waiting to strike you down when you mess up. I often wonder if this might be one of the most misunderstood verses in the Bible. My understanding is that God is within us, all around us, part of our life force, our light, and our energy field. I learned to recognize that which is within us as a higher power. [14]And God said unto Moses, "I AM THAT I AM: and he said, thus shalt thou say unto the children of Israel, "I AM hath sent me unto you.'" Exodus 3:14. Acknowledge, the "I AM," presence for your own life.

There is no room in the spiritual path for a victim role. Self-responsibility is scary, but empowering. When it comes to religion, people often worry what their friends and family might think of them. Don't worry about what other people think, God didn't make you, then choose you personally to pick on. The things that we have gone through do not define who we are. We learn (hopefully that our past does not define our future. We can avoid certain things and change our circumstances; it's one of the most empowering things that we can do. For some, (including myself) we grew up in darkness so we can understand and bring light; to others; we are consciousness. "I AM."

Ego. Dr. Wayne Dyer says in *Your Erroneous Zones*; EGO is an acronym for Edge God Out. Ego is driven by fear. Fear makes you question if you have enough compared to someone else. The ego is responsible for those upgrades you thought you needed because the neighbor had one and you wanted a better one. It is the voice inside your head that makes you feel that you are unloved, unworthy, and unhappy. It asks, "how can I profit from this" and seeks instant gratification. It's responsible for our spending, credit card debt, activities and interaction with humanity. You get the idea.

Negative thinking verses positive thinking. When you say, "I can't" your energies are manifesting and manipulating your environment so that you are correct, "You can't". When you say, "I can", you are also right, you are putting out to the universe the energy that it is possible to do this and manifesting events that draw the right people and places into your life that create the reality that "You Can." When you look at the word impossible, it is also actually saying, "I'm possible." Your self-limiting thoughts in your mind are your only limits to what is possible. When you say "I AM", you are connecting with God, you might even say the "God Particle", which helps in understanding the physics of space and properties of matter with regard to manifestation of your energy.

How do we manifest? Diet, walking, awareness, and meditation are part of the process. *The Secret* (Rhonda Byrne) tells us the first step in manifesting is to know what you desire or what you wish. Once we quit feeding the ego, we realize manifesting is not about "me". Becoming aware of the energy field around us is absolutely necessary to manifesting.

According to Philip Phalm: *Manifesting Manifesto,* we should have one major meal of the day about halfway in between waking and going to sleep at night. That point when we wake and before we eat our bodies are in a semi-fasting state. Phalm says the spirit adores a semi-fasting state and offers spirit the best access to our energies. Our accepting where we are right now in this moment is also essential. We must surrender and truly believe that which we want, it exists, and is beneficial to our being to obtain this energy. Learn that we have the innate ability to harness this field of energy to manifest our deepest energies. Prana (breathing exercises) or breath sustaining the body, helps apply nutrients to the body. Start tuning into your spiritual essence and become aware of your force field of energy that surrounds you. Wayne Dyer shared that prayers are when we talk to God and meditation is when God talks to you. He wrote, *Change Your Thoughts - Change Your Life.*

On Diet. Eat fundamental foods-protein, grains, nuts, seeds, and vegetables. When we eat the right food our solar plexus chakra is easily enhanced. When we have a "gut" feeling about something, we are usually right. Our gastrointestinal track is tied to solar plexus which is part of our emotional guidance system and how we feel about ourselves. Drink water, tea, and coffee. Avoid sugar, processed foods, and flour.

Do things to quit feeding the ego and let it become flaccid, placid, inactive, or dormant. Spending time in meditation is where we can focus our energies on receiving and raising our internal frequency. Activities such as taking long walks at daybreak or dusk, or along the water's edge is how we can begin to see that which is in our immediate presence. Living a simple life and eating a healthy diet; both require a certain amount of time, effort, and money and are certainly worth it in order to maintain the proper conditions for manifestation.

Empowerment. When we set the ego aside, we have the ability to connect with a higher consciousness of thoughts. We are able to receive an intuitive flow of guidance, and information, leading to higher prospective and higher vibration. The emotional conflicts in your life will need to be resolved so that they can be removed from your immediate conscious thoughts. This may necessitate you to part from some of your joys, friends, and family in order to make time for the walks and/in meditation. When meeting the proper criteria these conscious actions you have taken will intuitively bring about an environment where positive manifestation can occur.

How we know it's working. Small things begin to resolve. Life directions are laid out for your future. Your spirit moves into a magnetic framework circulation that draws others who are intended to help. Energy flows where attention goes (James

Arthur Ray, *The Secret,* 2006). People **change** their focus from present circumstances to what they desire. As a result of the actions where your energy goes, prosperity flows. Closing Remarks. Guilt and fear, when you live in this discipline, you realize it is a complete illusion. Only live in this illusion if you desire some form of pain. Wealth, power, and fear operate at low vibration. Raise your vibrations to a place of love, openness to enlightenment so you can absorb aspects of prosperity from a place of peace, inner consciousness, and self-awareness.

Sherri grew up in Mississippi and is a proud mother of two girls. She has a Bachelor's of Science in Psychology, has been a nurse for over twenty years, and has her MSN degree. Sherri is a Marine Corps veteran. She is an author in an anthology, Second Acts. When not working as a nurse she enjoys writing, traveling, and spending time with her two rescue miniature Yorkshire Terriers.

# Fred & Ingrid Edwards

**The Voice of Freedom**

Everyone has a voice but not everyone's voice is heard. The voice of my daughter had been hidden until the night after a silent storm. Much of her voice was silent. She would not talk at all and her responses was limited to yes or no that was coupled by rocking motions and blank stares. The morning after the storm, her voice became clear. She uttered words that still ring in my spirit today. She articulated to us that my 17-year-old son had sexually abused her, by the grace of God there was no penetration. Her voice that morning became as clear as a war call.

We cannot explain to you the feelings that we felt at that very moment. When we received the news that devastated us to the point of feeling internal death, we were joyous and angered at the same time. My Lord, it was a terrible situation that we struggled to accept but we knew that we had to be the hero to both of our children. We no longer had to be the voice for our daughter, she had found a way to articulate her storm to us. We too found a voice. In our minds, we were hoping that this was a mistake but in the midst of her words we heard a different voice, we heard the voice of freedom.

Late in the night while everyone was sleeping, our foster son that had never been adopted went into the bedroom of our five-year-old autistic daughter to have a night of satisfaction. Everyone in the house was sound asleep during the night hours. He would request sexual favors that no five-year-old could imagine. She was a girl of strength because she didn't rush to ask the aide of anyone at that time, although we often wish she would have screamed, she did not. She went through that night alone like most victims of sexual abuse. In the midst of the night, she found the words that she would tell my other two sons, her dad and I the next morning when the sun arose.

She came to breakfast and she spoke. She had not been able to articulate much to us since talking age. She quickly articulated to my two sons that she had been made to perform oral sex on my 17 year- old-son. In disbelief that this had occurred, my two sons rushed to tell me what they sister told them at the breakfast table. My daughter then spoke that she was made to perform oral sex on her old brother. The fact that she could tell us this without hesitation blew our mind. We were in unbelief. We were shocked and disgusted. She had never been able to tell us anything let alone tell us anything about sex. We knew it was the truth without hesitation and that we had to confront him directly with her present. Not shortly after talking with our other two sons and our daughter, we called my son downstairs to articulate what we were told by our five-year-old daughter.

My husband carried the rest of the children away for the day while my daughter, son, and I started to talk. We talked about last night. He must have been afraid because his first response to a question was a lie. Traumatized by his lies, my daughter screamed, "No, you are lying!" I quickly inserted that what he did was unacceptable and that she was telling the truth and that he was lying. He walked away angry and went into another room to get breathing room. While he was gone I would have to explain to my daughter that it was not her fault and that what happened to her was wrong. In a short amount of time he returned to where my daughter and I was located. With tears in his eyes, he confessed.

The power of his confession shook up the darkness. I cannot articulate to you fully the amount of relief and burden it brought to me. He then asked, "where do we go from here?" I quickly responded with faith, "we pray and then we call the police." I could see the fear in his eyes but I could see the freedom of every person that had been silenced because they were a victim of sexual abuse.

After prayer, we called the police. In a short amount of time they arrived at our house. The house was surrounded by constables, sheriffs and other officers. The police entered in and searched my foster son. They then questioned him about the reported incident and they even questioned my daughter. Afraid that she had lost her voice, I tried to speak for her, but she had indeed found her voice and still was able to tell the officers what occurred the night before. Still in disbelief, I was hurt by what occurred, I even felt shame but I knew that I was doing right by both my son and daughter. My son had to learn that there are consequences to all actions and my daughter had to know that I would protect her at all cost. To me, I protected both, I loved them both in that moment. I loved my son enough to correct him and let him suffer punishment, I loved my daughter enough for her to witness justice and freedom.

After much of the day, the police called the district prosecutor to take the case involving the sexual assault of a five-year-old. My son was then handcuffed and carried off to jail. My daughter had found her voice at the price of her innocence. I was left dealing with a child that had to deal with the emotional distress of being wounded, but she bounced back. Some days I often ask myself is this the girl that I brought home at 3 weeks old, she was having withdrawals symptoms because she had been birthed through a drug addict. My foster son would go on to be tried and prosecuted as an adult. He was charged with super aggravated assault of a child which could pull 25 years because she was only 5 and he was 17. He did in fact prey on her because of her condition.

What he thought would be a silent night forever would become an echo in his spirit forever. The words of my daughter echoed in his ear from that morning on. He would serve years in prison for one decision. Isn't it something how we can make one decision that affects us for the rest of our lives. Not only did I have to deal with the decision my son made, I had to live with the decisions I chose to make because of his choice on that night. As parents you don't stop loving your children when they do wrong, you let them work through their consequences but you never stop loving them. My son would never be allowed back home around any children, with the money earned from our upcoming books, we plan to donate all earnings to a charity that assist with housing for first time offenders and allowing them to learn job trades, gain counseling, and other needed skills to reintroduce them to the community.

I found freedom in my daughter's voice. I found freedom in her words. I was locked in embarrassment and shame. I was locked in a fear of rejection. Most of that night would have been my fault if I had silenced her, but I didn't, I couldn't! I knew her voice was a voice of freedom and that her cry would set everyone free on that day. My fear was failing as a parent and to many I had failed, but not to my daughter. She found her voice, she found her freedom. This is what being a parent is all about, it is about helping your children to find their voice in the world. Their words will echo throughout all generations. There are many voices that they will find, many voices they will encounter.

 My son chose a voice too, his words reverberated in courts and prisons. My daughter chose the voice of courage. Her voice is circling around for all those children that are struggling to find their voice because of autism. She is an example to them and to the life of all parents wondering if their child will ever speak. It was a voice of hope. I found a voice. My voice could not be silenced. My voice freed me from guilt and shame. It freed me from condemnation. I was bound by blame the night after that silent storm. I had taken kids in my home that had more than likely been sexually assaulted themselves. Was I stupid? I knew the chances and the repercussions of what bringing in wounded children could possibly do to my household. In that moment that I heard the news, I knew that I had to stand. I had to grow and break out of shame, I did not hesitate to quit the process after he apologized, I had seen this too many times. I was certain that if I freed him from consequence, I would bind my mind to guilt for the rest of my life. I chose the voice of freedom! I chose courage! So, if you are struggling to tell your story, I pray that you find your voice.

That you will discover purpose and meaning in all of life. That you will rise above the opinions of others and lean on God. That there would be no shame in any story. My hope is that everyone struggling with their voice, finds it. That they find their voice through the midst of trials and tribulations. That they discover their purpose in life and that they would not be silenced by fear. That those that have been silenced by family members too ashamed to speak on the matter of sexual abuse and incest would find a place in their heart to be free from shame. I pray that everyone will have the courage to reveal what is hidden in the secret places of the heart and echo the voice of freedom.

# Elizabeth Blade

**Find Your Freedom**

Sometimes within us all we have a fear that grows, we can have self-doubt and lack of confidence.
We also question our ability and ourselves. I have struggled over the years with confidence and from a very young age I was bullied in school, and although it felt like there was no end in sight, it lasted for years, all the way up until high school.
Now I am a grown woman in my thirty's and even now I get the oddball gossiping behind my back and dragging my name through the dirt. But how can one pick themselves up when the inner emotions deep inside of you are filling up with doubt?

From Fear to freedom is what we can learn over time. I always used to fear what others thought of me or what they felt towards me. Now, I realize that I was looking for others validation to validate myself. We sometimes look to others for their thoughts and opinions so we can feel better about our own self.

But at the end of the day we need to create a better mindset in how we feel, in how we see ourselves. We live with our own thoughts every single day. If we have had put downs, or feel negative then we will feel negative. But we must look for the world of positivity.

Through the hourglass is the sand and time runs out very quickly, we live our daily lives thinking about how others feel and sometimes we forget the bigger picture. How we feel ourselves. We must adapt a different way of thinking, a healthy mind of goodness works a lot better than a bad mind filled with sadness and heartache.

Everyone has experienced hardships in life. Whether it would be losing a loved one, being bullied in school, ending a friendship or whatever the situation. We somehow in some way have to get over it. We climb the hill; we reach the peak. The climb can be hard we somehow get over the mound and find the solid ground.

We made it! Then tragedy faces us again but each time we face the emotions. Sometimes we try and hide those feelings but underneath the surface is where they remain, again and again. We come across battles in life but whether we turn ourselves to the master of faith, love and divinity; we somehow overcome the hardships of it all.

I have been through things in life that has made me ponder how I got through it all. Stresses of everyday life can really get to you. Financial hardships, illness, society and the news of war and bloodshed all over the world can consume a person with deep thoughts of depression and anxiety, the feeling of absolute helplessness.

We all have to grip onto faith and find a way. Whatever way that works so we can find ourselves on the other side of sadness. We all want to be happy in life; we all want to find our way and make something of ourselves. That's what we need to do day by day.

Say the words you long to hear. Say the words to people's ears. That it will be okay. We can climb that mountain, however hard the climb, just keep on climbing and have the faith and love in your heart that you can do this. That we can face the better days and have so much better tomorrows. Whenever you feel like you are in fear just find the freedom from within.

> Have faith, I know I do.
> Love yourself.
> Free Yourself.
> Better Yourself.
> Be Yourself.
> Chase away the Fear and find your freedom.

Born in Melbourne Australia and raised in Adelaide, South Australia Elizabeth Blade has been one thing all of her life and that has been a dreamer. Elizabeth is in the middle of writing a variety of novels and books for all ages.

Through the years Elizabeth has written poetry, she believes that it has helped her overcome some troubling times in her life. Her first release that was debut in April of 2015 was an eBook called In Motion With Devotion Volume One more are to follow as each volume will be something new and a change of pace in various topics. Elizabeth will have a re-release of her book A Rising Moon on Domestic Violence set the be released in later 2016. Domestic Violence is in every corner of the globe. Through experiences witnessed or feelings that have delved inside due to media attention and news stories, Elizabeth decided to write a book about this. As a strong advocate that wants to see an end to this mindless violence she is determined to have her voice heard.  Elizabeth Blade is also an International Best Seller for a co-authored piece that she is extremely proud of.

elizabethblade.com;
moondance_81@me.com,
**Twitter**: @Moondance

# Duwanda S. Epps

**Years of Bondage, Ultimately Forgiveness lead to my Freedom**

From the age 4, I was held captive of graphic frightening images and cries of my mother that remain in my head. The replaying memories of my parents arguing and fighting. The horrible fights that left scars, scratches, bruises and bloodshed. Too many early mornings to remember running out to call the police from payphones. Shaken and totally afraid. Nervousness consumed my mind with anxieties and fear.

At the age 15, was my first experience of Domestic Violence, when my boyfriend tried to strangle me because I refused to answer his question. I recall other incidents of being choked, almost thrown down a flight of stairs, being pushed into glass, in which glass fragments are still in my body.

Countless fights that left bruised and scratches on my body, neck and face. I ran away one time because I was upset that an incident that goes on at my grandmothers. I sought shelter with my father. That stay was shortened due to being sexually touched by the one I totally trusted and assumed who would always protect me.

After, being sexually abused for third time I was angry and become weary. I was confused and questioned why this was happening to me by men I loved and respected. I attempted to take my own life by consuming a hand full of pills. Not to know the Lord was going to spare my life.

At the age of 25, one early morning I was awakened by the father of my children with things from the past and when I refused to engage in that conversation, he became so furious. I did not want to participate and in fact I decided to get dressed leave at 5:00 am. When he saw that I was about to leave, I could see him getting angrier and because I did not want to be in the same room he was in and I did not want to fight. He snatched my clothing from me as I was trying to get dressed, then pushed me onto the sofa, straddled his self on top of me and put a .22 caliber handgun to my head. I repeated the dysfunctional and abusive cycle as my mother did. I battled with other traumatic and emotional events in my life involving betrayal, being a homeless pregnant teen, a miscarriage and unwanted sexual advances. I had parents who did the best they could while both battling demons of addiction. I matured early to assist with my younger sisters.

I thought crying was a sign of weakness, so I refused to cry holding all my feelings to myself and hiding bruises and other pain with a smile. For about a decade my ex-husband told me I was stupid and I had issues. The physical, emotional, social and mental abuse I dealt with for all those years would build up and become the deepest valley I have ever walked through. Becoming a mother and role model to three children was my purpose and determination to want more out of life. I would not let them go through what I did, so I turned my pain into my passion to become a better individual and a great mother.

Through this transition, I learned to love myself more than any human can attempt to say. I trusted in my courage to take a stand for not only myself but my children. I believed in myself and acknowledged my worth. I walked by faith and not by sight relocating to NC when I completed my Master's degree in 2005. I was a single mother of 3 children and I was 25 years old. Demonstrating not only strength but determination by achieving goals I have set for myself.

I dedicated over a decade serving different communities. I love teaching my children the importance of hard work, teamwork, respect, responsibility and accountability. From a child I remember teachers and other professionals telling me I have a calling to inspire others. All in which I from early on I've tried to avoid. I despised speaking aloud. Afraid and embarrassed of my difficulties with punctuating words correctly. But who would've thought this incorrect voice had a story to tell, a voice that needs to be heard and a message to deliver.

I realize that I endured all I did for reason. My expression of thoughts using pen and paper as an outlet to express my life experiences. The determination to use those reflections as stepping stones to heal and overcome past pains and struggles.

On September 2015, the Lord spoke to me and that day I launched EEL: Enchained, Exculpate, Liberate Movement- Broken Silence supporting DV & SA. As Philippians 4:13 reads "I can do all things through Christ who strengthens me."

### My personal message to all:

*Be the Creator of your Destiny; Unveil your Purpose!*

*-Author D S. Epps*

*Pain can promote positive change #Roc'On#UrWorthy#*

- ✓ A strong woman is one who is able to smile this morning like she wasn't crying last night.
- ✓ You can break down a real woman temporarily but a real woman will always pick up the pieces, rebuild herself and come back even stronger than ever.
- ✓ A woman is the full circle. Within her is the power to create, nurture and transform.

Author DuWanda S. Epps    Known as D S. Epps

Aside from being a Wife for the second time, a new Mother of a precious surprise and 4 other growing children, Notary since 2007, Author of 9 books, including a new-released book, "Tre'Zure Box" (erotica), "Flowin Emotions," "Flowin Emotions ll" (self-help books). #1 Bestselling author in 2 new released books, "Pain 2 Passion: Our Valley Experience" and "Chocolate & Diamonds: Celebrating the Majesty of Motherhood."

I am one of the founders of (EEL) Roc'On Ur Worthy Movement: Joining together to educate, empower and prevent DV and SA against women and men. Taking courage, strength and faith to take a Stand. Non for Profit Cultivating Change II, Inc (2010) assisting families in the community in need of clothing, food, household items and providing resources in the community for additional services and assistance & Cultivating Change, LLC (2008). Launching of Epps CreativeMindz Enterprise this May, 2016 providing reasonable services for small businesses, authors, entertainers and all others with effective marketing and publishing services for their business or brand.

Awards & Additional Achievements include:
- 2016-2017 One Warm Coat
- 2015-2016 One Warm Coat
- 2014-2015 One Warm Coat
- 2015 receiver of a letter from Women's Battered Shelter in North Carolina.
- 2012-2013 Better Business Bureau Award:

- KidzCorner Art
- 3 year Adopt a family for Christmas.
- 15-year list of other asset to the community in the Eastern Carolinas and New York contributions.
- One of 17 brave women who opened up about their past hurt. Another enlighten, encourage and empowering reading for both men and women globally to show the world that we have turned our pain into #PASSION and #PURPOSE!

My passion to serve and service the community for long over a decade. Myself and another Author with the same interest in serving and advocating are initiating a library project for women shelters in our city. Our desire is to provide resilient empowerment stories in the shelters to empower and equip survivors during their transition. To be an empowerment when thoughts are present go to going back to their unhealthy relationships, at this crossroad. Our books can be a pillar to assist them to be strong and help keep them moving in a healthy direction.

This project is embraced for My EEL Movement: Enchained (held Captive) *Exculpate (verb Forgive) *Liberate (Freedom).
I have asked other Authors who supports taking a stand for DV and SA. To assist our Empowering Library authors must donate (1) book per participating shelter with envisioning recognition in their name.
Upcoming Projects includes:3 Anthologies- 1. Redefining Sisterhood, Daily Inspirational Devotion (2017) and Single Fathers Journey, I have a Heart. Children's Poetry "Rhymes & Reasons (2016)- An young author entrepreneurship opportunity project.

Short Film/ Documentary:
A short film about an African American woman's story of triumph, abuse, and faith. The main character witnesses' domestic violence as a child, then grows up to be in a violent

relationship herself. She also experiences sexual abuse as well as being a homeless pregnant teen. Her broken marriage leads to a near drug overdose. Despite the hurt and pain, she is able to graduate high school, college and earn a Master's Degree at the age of 25. A world of struggles did not keep her from being the woman and living the life destined for her. With compassion to empower, embrace and strengthen women & families for 15 plus years. I am presently a project fund for Women Rebuilding & Transforming to provide 6-12 months of Life Coaching Services FREE to women rebuilding & transitioning in life and/or from battered shelters. My goal is to provide resilient empowerment and supportive outreach to promote self-sufficiency.

http://www.plumfund.com/crowdfunding/eel-movement-sister-2-sister
I am a Survivor of domestic Violence & Sexual Abuse!
www.flowinemotions.weebly.com
www.linkedin.com/in/authordseppswww.eppscreativemindenterprise.comwww.authordsepps.com
Twitter: FlowinEmotions
authordsepps@outlook.com

# Raffine' LaJuan

**Against All Odds**

It's odd how things work out in your favor. Against all odds I was determined to win. Much like a marathon, I ran the distance. My journey began at an early age, although I was still not legally an adult, I often felt like one. The old people always told me I had an old soul. This was destiny for me, much of my journey had often seemed like a mistake, but it was not, I believe it was not an accident. I had many fears, one being failure. Fear of not being enough, fear of being a statistic, a fear of not finishing what I started. I was determined to win because that was all I knew! At the age of 15, I was pregnant with my first son. I was tested in so many ways and was determined not to be a statistic. They said I would not make it out of high school, let alone college. This all determined what I was made of. My story did not end there; I would rewrite it several times. Just when most counted me out, I counted myself in because I knew that I was a champion.

As the eldest sibling, I took on the role of a leader. My life was consisted of leading my siblings in a respectful manner. They saw me struggle and they saw me succeed but I had no excuses. I was free to move and do things the way that I wanted. I led by example. Much of my life can be compared to a marathon, all I had was endurance. My childhood was consistently normal until the year that I found out I was with child. The feeling that I felt the moment that I found out the news was one of great strength but I knew that it would come with great adversity. I knew that my life would change forever. I would not give up without a fight, I would accomplish many things from what many deemed as a mistake. My first son was the fuel to my fire, he pushed me to succeed. I told my boyfriend the news of our pregnancy, he was determined to be a good father. He was a high school football star that had many other girls looking for him to talk to them. I was not intimidated by his high school superstardom, I just wanted him to do right by his son and I for the duration of our relationship. I believed the best about the situation and was determined to do what I had to do.

The heart of a winner is always to train hard now and to finish strong. After the first and second trimester, things were hopeful. I still attended school on a daily basis. I was excited to learn that I could fight by myself through anything. I went to school sometimes ashamed but other times knowing that I was blessed to have a healthy baby growing inside of me. Not shortly before the baby was due I was devastated to find out that my boyfriend had gotten one of my friends pregnant. We would have babies within months of each other. The girl was a friend of the family and also attended the same high school as us. I was shocked by the drama that soon exploded in my life but was not moved. Shortly after finding out that my friend was pregnant by my boyfriend the same time that I was, I began to question things in my life.

The questioning of where I was going and what I wanted to do added more fuel for me to finish my race. I was not going to force him to commit to me, I was committed to myself. I committed to finishing my race strong. I was committed to graduating high school on time. I was committed to being a light to my family. I told my siblings that if I could finish, they could finish all the more. You know, sometimes things are allowed to happen in life in order for it to serve as fuel to get you to your next destination. I believe that in the midst of the adversity I was facing, I had the attitude of a champion. In spite of being the talk of the school and having drama weekly in high school, I finished strong and went on to college. I would not be a statistic in the black community, I was running my race with endurance. At 17, my boyfriend and I decided to get married and tried to make our relationship work. Although he had made many mistakes while we were dating, I continued to try and not give up on him.

During that time, things would continue to get worse. We stayed married for three years and not shortly after that, we would decide to depart from each other lives for a season. I was disappointed but having the mindset of a victor. I continued to press my way to the finish line. Although I was determined to finish my race, I would still experience many heartaches and bruises. I believe that just like in a race, you may fall, you may scrap your leg and bruise your arm, your legs may cramp, but if you focus on the end, you will finish strong. I would not play the victim in any of my circumstances because I knew that there was always a way out.

While in college I secured a high paying job with benefits, 401k, and salary. I carried my baby on my hip to classes in the evenings and during the summers with small break in-between. I want you to know that if you set a goal, you can finish it. All your need is a plan. I finished school in 2 and a half years all while managing a household as a single parent. I did have the support of family but was determined not to depend on anyone except myself.

My strength was great because I accomplished my goal by graduating in 2007 from the University of North Texas with my degree in business. After finishing college, I would secure an even better job within my field in no time. This is what God does for those that refuse to quit, he makes it seem like you never went through anything. It was a big deal for me to continue on as one of the top employees in my field. I would keep working and securing deals while managing as a single parent. I then got pregnant again and would have another son that would be a blessing to me and my eldest son. This was another trying time but again I would prove that with God, all things were possible.

I learned to depend on God as a source of my strength whenever I needed help. This too was a way I finished my race. While working as a career woman, I fell into running. Running was not on my list of things to do but after a co-worker told me that I should take run with them during a lunch break, I decided to join the party. As I was running, I soon felt tired but knew that I had to make it back to my car and be back at work before a certain time. It was finish or get fired! I pushed myself until the end because I knew I could not afford to lose my job. When I completed that long distance run, I felt accomplished but most importantly, I felt like it was my purpose. From that day forward I began to run daily until I became a professional runner. I quit my day job to train and run for a living. This is a testament that things will always work out for us if we stay true to who God created us to be.

As a professional runner, I now live the life many only dream about living. I run for fun and I run for purpose. I am a sponsored runner that loves training. A runner was always in me because I never gave up. I would always endure until the end. No matter how tired I get, I have to finish! Against all odds, I am a victor. Much of the work I do now is training others not to quit. I train others to develop the attitude I had when I was faced with heartache, teen pregnancy, school and work as a single mother, I RAN! I ran the race with endurance even though I felt the burns of disappointments. I ran! Just like the bible says, the race is not given to the strong nor to the swift but to the one that endures until the end! So, if you are single mother or you a woman faced with adversity, if you feel like giving up, do not quit. ENDURE! While you are enduring you will find your purpose and passion and you will finish the course that is set for you. Run and win like a victor, against all odds!

Raffinae' LaJuan Dallas, Texas native and proud mother of two amazing young men, Tederail III and Logan. She is a

Professional Distance Runner, Motivational Speaker, Life Coach, Founder & Brand Ambassador for Moms for Medals

The purpose for Moms for Medals is to encourage, empower, inspire, and motivate one person at a time to life. In hopes they will take it back to their own world and affect the people in their community and home. Many operate with their physical sight, so we offer fitness empowerment /education & life coaching. Our mission is to unlock their spiritual sight which allows them to be moved in such a way that no matter what it looks like, what people say or think, what their family history dictates, that through a collective story and experience be the catalyst to empower them to reach higher heights, conquer fears that they never thought imaginable.

# Nakia P. Evans

**My Personal Freedom**

I'll never forget the feeling of having the barrel of a gun pressed to my right temple. I closed my eyes in prayer that I would get another chance to see my daughter, who was only 3 at the time. I prayed to a God that I only knew of, but didn't really know for myself. I prayed to Him that I would get another chance to see her smile and to hear her laugh. I pictured her in my mind as the fear of dying took over me. I wasn't ready to go. I was only 23! I felt like I still had so much to do and so much to give.

There were still goals and dreams that I had that I wanted to accomplish. The tears began to fall harder as I seen the look in his face. I knew at that moment, that this was it for me. I knew that I would no longer be here anymore. I closed my eyes and took a deep breath and I realized that there was no place to run and no place to hide. I realized that the life I was currently living was not the life I truly owned. The last moments of this life was about to end. CLICK! BAM!

Growing up, I encountered a lot of things that made my self-esteem drop very low! At the age of 7, I was molested by a family member. It was then that I began thinking that something had to be wrong with me. As a young child, I felt like my world was bright and so full of life. However, after that event, my world became dull, dark, and grey. I began covering and pretending who I was. I didn't want people to see the real me, which was broken, hurt, abused, and abandoned. I wish I could say it was a one-time event, however, it wasn't. My molestation lasted from the ages of 7-13. Many times I felt myself wanting to commit suicide. The way I looked at myself changed. I didn't see myself worthy. I didn't see myself as beautiful. What I saw was a damaged young girl who was abused and neglected in every way. I saw a young girl who wasn't believed; who wasn't protected. All I knew was that I needed and longed for someone to come and rescue me.

I found different ways with coping with my pain. I began getting into crowds that I honestly didn't need to be in. These crowds led to me drinking and smoking at a young age. I figured that if I hung out with the "cool kids", then no one know or see my pain. My grades dropped. My attitudes changed. I didn't care about hurting others because no one cared about my hurt. No one cared about my pain. It is a known fact that hurt people only hurt other people, and that is exactly what I did. My pain spoke out in every word and every action. After all, how was I supposed to deal with it. There was no counseling. There were no conversations. In fact, as a kid, I just had a wide imagination, as I was told. I found myself getting into crazy relationships. I would date dangerous guys who I felt like they would protect me at any cost. They seemed like tough guys and I felt like that is the type of person I needed in my life, because if they are that tough, and they truly care about me, then they would protect me from feeling that pain again. Little did I know; it was the complete opposite.

I met a young man in my Sophomore Year in College. I was already a Single-Mom. I met him through a few of my friends. He seemed very nice. He was a street guy so he hustled and had money. He spoiled me rotten and I got anything I ever wanted. He made me feel like I was the Queen of the world. I began distancing myself from my friends because I felt like they didn't understand what I needed in my life. After All, they didn't truly know the pain I dealt with anyways. I felt like I was adored and loved. I felt like I was happy and that I had finally found someone to truly love me. That didn't last long.

The abuse started verbally. He would say different things about me that would hurt my feelings. I was so lost into trying to please him that I would change how I dressed and would change my hair. Then things became physical. At first it started with a slap, then it escalated. Hitting me and calling me names seemed to be amusement for him and his friends. Instead of being what I thought I was, I found myself to be so much less. I learned that the strength I portrayed, seemed to be something that he didn't like. If he would hit me, it was best for me to stay down and not get up.

I will never forget the day I knew my life would end. I was at the house sitting in the chair. A small conversation escalated into a heated argument. I saw his hand reach for his gun, which wasn't anything new to me. I always knew it existed. I saw it every day. It was a constant part of my daily life with him. What I did not expect is the gun to be pointed at me. The look in his eyes was different. My heart started pounding as I tried to get up and leave. I managed to get outside the door and to the side of my car. My hands shook as I tried to put the keys in to unlock the door. That didn't work. He grabbed me and pushed me up against the car. One hand was around my throat and the other was holding the gun that was pressed to my head. I could feel the barrel pressed forcibly to my head.

The tears started to fall. The fear I felt that day could never be matched to any other fear I've ever had. My mind began to wonder how I got here. I replayed my journey to this moment. I was fearful of losing life. The biggest question was that was it truly MY life? I had become someone I didn't know. Yes, the pain was real. Yes, the pain was deep, but who was the person I had become because of it? In a matter of a second, this life that I thought was mine could be over. I realized that I didn't truly value life the way I should have. I did crazy things to feel "cool" and to mask the hurt and pain that I was feeling. Here I stood at 23 years old, trying to fight and save a life that I didn't truly own. This wasn't the life God had planned for me. It isn't the life that I truly wanted to live. I didn't really want to be this person. I just needed to pretend to fit in to mask who I truly was, which was hurt.

BAM! I heard the gun go off and when I opened my eyes, I was still standing by my car. I can gladly say that on that night, I did experience death. Even though the trigger wasn't pulled in my direction as I first thought, a part of me died. I experienced death of the life I tried to live.

That night, I learned that life can end so quickly without any notice. I stopped doing many of the things I were doing and I learned that there was something I could fight. I learned that there was something worth having, and that was ME. I had to start fighting for me. I had to understand that this life that God has given me was worth living. So as a part of my life died, a new life began to take place. I stopped hanging around the same crowds. I stopped participating in the things that I once did. Gladly, I can say that I stopped dating the "Street Guys" and started valuing my life more that I was before.

We must understand that many times we live a life that we truly don't own. I couldn't own that life, because it wasn't who I was. It wasn't who God had for me to be. It was a life that I took and pretended to live. This experience has taught me that the girl I once say as unworthy, Is truly worthy! No matter what life has ever thrown you, your true life is worth fighting for!

Nakia P. Evans, The Authentic Living Strategist, is the Founder/ CEO of Authentically You and Authentically You Magazine. She is also the Radio Host of Real Talk with Kia Radio, Ladies Table Talk Radio, and Insight Radio. She is also the founder of Woman, Unmask Yourself Movement.

Nakia began her journey in Broadcasting in college at Morris College in Sumter, SC. She completed her Senior Internship at WLJI, Gospel 98.3 under the leadership of Program Director/Radio Personality, Nate Stoney. She also worked at 95.3 in Columbia, SC. After graduating from college in 2007, Nakia began working at the Camden Chronicle Independent Newspaper. She then moved to work independently under the leadership of the late Mr. Larry Adamson of Gospel Line Magazine.

Nakia always had a passion for Broadcasting. In September 2013, She began her Radio Talk Show, Real Talk with Kia Radio, which airs live on each Monday at 7 PM EST. This radio program has grown tremendously in the last 2 1/2 years. Nakia has had the pleasure of interviewing many great names such as Micheal Baisden, from 100.1 BIG DM, Pastor Wess Morgan, Joshua Rogers, Alexis Spight, Tasha Page-Lockhart, Tony Grant, Tyler Perry Staff, and many more! After dealing with many struggles in her life, Nakia knows what it feels like to be masked, covered, hidden, and abandoned. It is her passion and vision to help empower women to embrace who they truly are. To know what their Father and Creator has said about them! Nakia helps women unmask and face those things that are hindering them! Woman, Unmask Yourself!

# Aneisha Rush LeMonier

**There is Hope**

When I was having those "little girl dreams" about what I wanted to be when I grew up, it definitely did not include pregnant at 16, divorced at 29, involved in a domestic abuse relationship, battling anxiety and more or less homeless. No, those categories were foreign to my dreams. But they were my reality. One thing for sure, if you do not set boundaries and goals for yourself, someone else will establish them for you. In the midst of this 20 plus year "unfolding," there were two things hidden deep in my arsenal of tools that didn't get lost along the way. The first was my Dad. A man who had seen his fair share of adversities and obstacles in his 74 years, and my mind that didn't quit imagining a better way, an easier life, and continued dreaming in my darkest moments.

Even though I dropped out of school at the age of 15, and then again at 17, it was not because I lacked intelligence or drive. Far from it. The teen pregnancy had me deathly ill most of the term of the pregnancy, and then my maternal instincts fired up when I held my son, Matthew (which means gift from God), and I struggled with leaving him with anyone. Fortunately, there were educators and administrators in my school system who looked beyond my situation and circumstances and incessantly challenged me to return and earn my diploma, and earn was definitely the right word! It was hard work, but I graduated with straight A's in May of 1984.

In 1997, my world changed again as my relationship to my son and daughter's Dad deteriorated and ended in divorce. At the age of 31 I was a single mother with two young children, and earning $7.50 an hour. My skills were minimal as I had not really held a job that would develop any. Waitressing and babysitting definitely fell in the "hard work" arena, but it was not impressive on a resume. What other options were there for a single mom? Tentatively I entertained community college. Then, before I knew it, those moments of checking things out unfolded and found me enrolled as a full time student.

Thankfully most of the memories of shut-off utilities, bounced checks, crying myself to sleep, fighting depression, studying into all hours of the night and morning, and working more waitressing jobs, are all a blur in my mind. Thrown in to this mix were the common frustrations and disillusionments found in the majority of communications that would involve ex-spouses. Definitely not the childhood I desired, or dreamed of, for my children who were the world to me. The emotions were always vacillating between high and low with very few coasting points.

Even though I was the first person in my family to attend, and graduate college, the event came and went without any celebration or "fuss" being made. It just happened. Slowly but surely as my exposure to other women in leadership positions occurred at college, and I met other non-traditional students, my confidence started to develop. I really thought I could "be someone" one day. Then I met a man who thought I could too! Wind beneath my wings… I was elated to be validated and seen finally, and all by a man I thought was very intelligent with his two engineering degrees and background of traveling the world!

Fairytales. Even though I thought I was finally being introduced to one in real life, it actually became more in-line with a Grimm's fairytale instead. Jekyll and Hyde could easily describe the two juxtaposed personalities dwelling inside my partner. His mood changes and anger were as severe as his love and adoration was comforting. This unstable pattern did not make me run screaming in the opposite direction, but instead made me question what I could do differently to prevent the "switch" to begin with.

It is amazing the subtleties which start shaping your life, which are all based on fears instead of dreams and aspirations. There came a time in my life I realized I quit smiling. This forced, unnatural grin took the place of my once natural smile. In my mind, the relationship that was eating away at my sanity and dreams was also the one thing I craved. In the years of gas lighting, manipulation, financial insecurity and emotional abuse, this was still my familiar setting in which I took responsibility for its brokenness. The other thing was my mindset, "my situation wasn't that bad...compared to others." Yes, this singular thought, and belief, provided my anchor to exist in a situation I should have run from. But, like I was informed by him, "Who would have me?"

November 2011, in Winnetka, IL, my mental ability to endure finally broke. The verbal, mental, physical and sexual abuse took its toll and my desire for freedom didn't look like me walking out the door and never looking back. No, it resembled a grown woman struggling to get into a bathroom, begging the abuser to quit, while opening a prescription of Xanax and swallowing nearly 30 pills and chasing it with as much vodka as I could. I relaxed. My battle was over, he won, and I would get relief from the constant abuse.

There is a very brief memory of being jostled by EMT workers rushing to get me to a hospital. My next brief recollection is 24 hours later and a young physician standing by my hospital bed asking, "I'm curious. Can you tell me why you wanted to die?" Although I was very lethargic, I was able to answer, "I didn't. I just wanted out and I can't fight him anymore." The young doctor truly appeared saddened by the mess which was me and my life...and I was too! He went on to inform me how lucky I was to be alive. I drifted back into oblivion.

My next recollection was waking in a mental hospital. Anxiety flooded me as I walked out of me towards the nurse's station to try and find answers to what was going on in chaotic life. Lord knows I was clueless. I was fortunate to get the attention of one very kind, very compassionate, beautifully large black lady who had an angelic smile and smelled amazingly just as nice! My angelic nurse tried to get me up to date on what had been happening in my life, as four days had passed. After she filled me on the details she knew, she pointed a finger at me and said, "I've been praying for you, young lady. God isn't done with you!" Her message went straight to my heart.

On November 14, 2011 I was finally discharged from the hospital as I convinced the psychologist I was fine, I would get help in my home state of Arkansas, and informed them I had no pay source. That last bit of information was probably the real kicker! Because I was in Chicago, 800 miles from home, I allowed myself to be discharged into the care of the one man who was the impetus of my desperation. In my mind I had no choice though. Who else was I to call in Illinois?

It was an uncomfortable and sad situation and the drama failed to stop. The first night was okay, but the next night the fighting returned and resulted in me calling the police to escort me out to a safe place. I stayed in a hotel near the airport, thanks to the officers, and was able to get a taxi to O'Hare airport the next day, and flew back to Little Rock AR compliments of my aging parents who did not need this. I was defeated...but almost free.

From 2012, until 2013, many things took place to help me in the transformation from broken and ashamed, until now in my "complete and whole" stage. The journey was tough as I worked to unlearn the bad behavior styles of the past relationship, embracing the power of forgiveness towards my ex, and myself, and allowing my life to "meld" back into oneness of who I am, and who I was destined to be. This happened with the help of three very strong influences in my life. My new partner, friend, and husband, Tim, to whom I owe a huge thank you for my Cinderella Rescue, and gifting me with acceptance and the restoration of love.

Another influence was my Dad. He was dying. I became stronger as he became weaker because I knew he needed me, and I did not want to let him down anymore. I would not have another opportunity to give him the assurance I would be okay. The last influence, and definitely not the least, was a tree that stood all alone in my fenced-in field and allowed me to find amazing spiritual, and life lessons, in its existence.

I started to write a small amount of scripture and devotion material each morning to share on Facebook. Somehow "My Tree" moments grew and it now has its own album on my profile, and I have captured some spectacular sunrises, storms, cloud formations, and I saw the "Hand of God" in the simple things. This tree helped me as I stared out my window and sobbed missing my one constant in my life, My Dad and My Hero. He was now gone. He fought the good fight, he finished his race…with dignity and courage.

My dad was one who never complained in life of his childhood abuse, or wrestling with PTSD from the atrocities of the Vietnam War, or his deteriorating health and mobility which was directly linked to the Agent Orange used in that war. There were very difficult times as he endured a major stroke at the age of 40 and was paralyzed, and learned to walk, talk, and eat again. He finally became home bound in 2013 until he finally left this world 3 days after his birthday which was April 04, 2014. He died at the age of 74. Although my dad is gone, his legacy of hope marches on. I hear it in my own head, and it is resounding in my heart as well. You see, when dad was recovering from a surgery one day, and he and I were "jaw-jacking" (talking) as he liked to call it, he told me he wished he would have written a book about his life. I asked him, "What would you title this book Dad?" Without hesitation he replied, "Hope. There is Hope."

You may wonder how all of this pertains to anyone besides me. Great question! I think I have the answer for those who are questioning. Even though I am a firm believer in life after death, I was still very sad. Grief is a very tangible thing. I was longing to hear a loving voice who constantly encouraged me. My sadness was starting to creep in very heavily, and I knew I needed to do something. I found a direct sales company to get involved in to help me meet new women for friendship, and have something to take my mind off the loneliness. Who knew this one decision was going to be such a page turner for me, along with exposing me to social media and the power of reaching out to others and making a difference. I began to see "there is hope" for all of us.

When you join a direct sales company, they usually have "groups" for training, inspiration and motivation to add you to. That was the case here as well. I started "showing up" in these groups, learning, encouraging others, making friends, feeling someone else's struggles, and extending that part of me which could instill in them the "HOPE" I so firmly believed in. Facebook became a platform for me to minister to others who were broken, broken-hearted, defeated feeling, and more than anything else… lonely. I truly felt their pain.

As my world broadened with new people, my direct sales skills started increasing as well. There is a quote by Zig Ziegler, "You can get everything in life you want if you will just help enough other people get what they want." I had no idea this was a philosophy I was living out, I only understood that so many others were feeling pain. I felt that pain, and knew when I was in pain, I wanted mine lifted… so I tried to alleviate someone else's too. No strings attached.

As I began my mornings for the first time looking at a lily from my Dad's funeral, and seeing that one lonely tree out in my field with the sun rising gloriously behind it, my soul began to heal from the abuses, the unanswered questions, and shame I wore around my own neck like a blazing emblem I thought everyone else could see. Time was marching onward, no longer backward, and I became a woman passionate to share hope, to make a difference in the lives of my family, my grandchildren, and those I would cross paths with for whatever reason. I finally understood three universal principles: "I was never alone," "I could not fail only learn," and the most important, "I was loved more than I knew" by a God who promised to never forsake me.

The beauty of this entire story, is it is no longer just mine. It is the story of so many who made me who I am, enabling me to be much stronger than I ever knew. Leaving a legacy is extremely important to me now. Very much so. A desire of my heart was to start a scholarship for those seeking to better themselves in my father's honor. As this story is being written, the birth of the "There is Hope" scholarship is occurring. Past network connections have allowed me an opportunity to redeem my career, and partner with a company who is taking the ceiling off of women's heads and allowing us to earn as much as any person...male or female.

One other thing they are doing that I think is amazing, is they are setting me up to form the There Is Hope Scholarship with a group of benefactors who are excited to be part of this story tragedies and hope. Looking back into my life I could easily be distracted by the storms and miss the rainbows, forget the cleansing of the rains that washed the earth and my life, and only focus on the rumbling thunder or sky-shattering lightening of certain events. It would be so easy to do, and there are support groups for those who can't, don't, or won't see the beauty and only see the pain. During the last 30 years there was plenty of that, but there is also so much more. There's my children...there's my grandchildren... there's my nieces and nephews, and my step-children who are the next generation of decision-makers... they need me to be present and able to help *them* up if they too stumble. I *AM* part of a circle that will not be broken. There is a hope in me that was sparked by Dad that needs to be passed on to the next generation.

Triumphs only happen when you are victorious over something, when a price, or sacrifice, takes place to remind you of how sweet the victory is! And it comes when faith, hope and love, all work together to bring us into the victory arena. I have not yet "arrived" in my final spot on this planet, but I am standing on solid ground in a loving marriage with a man who loves and honors me, and I am a Nana to five little monkeys who keep me laughing and on fire with love on the inside of my soul, and my involvement with direct sales keeps me plugged in to the THOUSANDS of women who are yearning to hear the message, "There IS hope."

After living in Texas, Alaska and Kansas, due to my Dad's military career, we finally retired to a small town nestled on the beautiful White River in Calico Rock, Arkansas in 1972. Growing up in the hills of Arkansas was quite an adventure as you were both safe from many outside influences, but yet sheltered from a world that did not resemble your own. But it was home, it was familiar, and I completely identified with Laura Ingles Wilder.

Outside of writing for our high school newspaper, *The Pirate*, my first published work was in the county paper, *The White River Current*, which is now known as *The Current*, and I reported on local events, meetings, and public interest segments. Because the pay was not the greatest, my career journey veered in to all things business, and I was an Executive Analyst for one of the largest and oldest consulting firms in Chicago.

In 2014, as my Dad's health deteriorated, and his days were obviously numbered, my career stood still. Then sorrow and grief became my constant companions, and once again I turned to writing for solace. Because we live in an age where phones are actually mini computers, my ability to write anywhere broadened my writing opportunities, and my passion once again became a source of income.

Connect with her at http://aneisha.com/

# Teresa Sisson

## "Drowning in a Sea of Grace"

Momma,

I miss you so much. I want to hear your voice; I want to spend the day doing everything or absolutely nothing as long as it is with you; I just miss you. I have so much to do now, because it seems that I am expected to take up your torch and carry on. Everyone is so sad and they are looking to me for answers; if they only knew how few answers I really have. I get up every day and try to meet their needs, try to make sure everyone is as okay as possible. I try to bridge the void you left, knowing I will never truly fill your shoes, but I'll never stop trying.

...the saddest part is all I really want to do is cry and everyone (including me) is trying to avoid that for fear I may never stop. If you were here I know I could lay my head in your lap and just cry from the most broken recesses of my heart. I would cry until there were no more tears, and you would let me. I miss you so very much, your absence is a physical ache I can't ease. Until we meet again know that I love you more than words can express."

5:26 on Saturday morning, May 14, 2016, life has changed forever; Daddy is on the front porch yelling about how Momma has "just up and died" in her sleep. "What?" is the single thought in my mind for the next few moments. Then it's my voice I hear screaming for my husband as I run next door to Momma. I need her to wake up; I need to wake up, because surely this is a nightmare. Unfortunately, there was no waking up there was just a new reality.

To be honest the first two weeks of this journey are almost a complete blur. It was a bit like watching a TV drama where you are completely invested in the character's lives but you remain a spectator. Within hours the house was filled with family and friends. Thousands of calls, texts, and media posts came in offering condolences, help, and prayers. Heaven was being flooded with prayers for strength, peace, and comfort and God was present. Every grain of faith was being called upon to just keep moving.

God showed up and showed out. Let me give you a little perspective on me: I'm that one family member who just loses it at every sentimental occasion (no sadness necessary) and here I was making decisions and getting things done. I even wrote and read my momma's eulogy. I had not one but three back-ups prepared to take over because we all assumed I was going to break down sooner rather than later. I didn't break.

I felt a strength I had never known; I was going through the days efficiently. There were arrangements to make, relatives to coordinate, people to console. I could literally feel God's Grace covering me. Having been raised in a faith based home I know the power of prayer, but I had never felt anything like this. Now that's not to say that I was on autopilot; I would go home late at night, crawl into bed, snuggle up next to my hubby and allow myself to have a mini meltdown and just miss my momma. I was insulated in God's Grace, so much so that even I was wondering what was wrong with me. My dearest friend, my biggest fan, my hero was gone... Why wasn't I hysterical?

This was a question haunting the edges of my mind. I fell asleep one night and had what felt like the most vivid dream.

The Lord came and told me that what I was feeling was answered prayers. He said, "you asked for peace, comfort, and strength. You had those around you ask the same for you. Why do you question the answer?" So, I stayed in prayer and got through the days that followed. The prayers of my family and friends were holding me up. The funeral came and it was hard, but all that pain gave way to a great celebration of Momma's life, then it was over, friends and family went home, and the world kept turning.

I'm not sure when I realized I was adrift in a vast ocean, but here I am none the less. Minutes turned into hours, hours turned into days, days turned into weeks and weeks are becoming months. I wish the thoughts were still so few as they were in the first moments. Instead there are so many thoughts I can hardly keep them straight. I do know that every day brings new challenges and new answers, lots of busy work.

The shoreline is nowhere to be seen. As I take on my new role in the family I notice that this ocean has no beginning and no end in sight. There are only waves of grief and it takes all my strength to keep my head above water. Sometimes it is nothing more than a ripple that disrupts my day for only a moment, but sometimes it is a tsunami threatening to sweep me away.

It's impossible to brace myself because I'm never sure which wave is coming, or when, or why, or how long I might be pulled under by it. I'm only aware of one simple truth; when the wave hits, the surface is my destination. I have to admit there have been moments where I struggle with the desire to let the wave take me: let the pain have its way and stop praying for God to bring me through.

Imagine my surprise when almost 2 months after Momma left I suddenly can't feel God's Grace! All I feel is anger and pain. As I stress out over my new **roles** and try keeping all the balls in the air, I am face to face with my grief. Yes, I miss

Momma terribly, in fact I think my heart physically hurts, but I know grief is a process and I will survive this storm in my soul. I keep telling myself these things and hoping they are all true. Friends offer support and my family is always here for me, but I feel isolated. I feel like the world is resting squarely on my shoulders.

Daddy says, "You need to go to the graveside and make peace with your Momma." Now this is not what I want to do; I have never found peace at a graveside, there is no comfort there for me. I went anyway, because I knew it would make Daddy feel better. When leaving I tune my radio to KSBJ and the announcer is telling the story of Peter walking on the water. A story most of us know, and how Peter only began to sink below the surface when he would take his eyes off of Jesus. Somewhere in the story I found my lifeline because I realized what is really holding me down. It's fear! I'm afraid, more afraid than I have ever been in my life. What if I can't do it all? What if the family falls apart, what if the girls need advice that I can't give? What happens when my abrasive personality gets in the way of comforting them the way Momma always comforted everyone? What if Daddy doesn't eat enough? What if I forget to pay the bills? What if I don't spend enough time with Daddy, Ronn, Amanda, Samantha, Sandra, Kim, Sheena, Granny, Aunt JoAnn? What if I neglect the very friends who I turned to just a few months ago? What if I can't don't, won't... What if?

Then I suddenly realized, I thought I was lost in an ocean of grief, but nothing could be farther from the truth. I am adrift in a sea of grace. I've been wondering why God removed His comforting blanket of Grace that He had covered me with during the first few days. Now I realize that He hadn't taken it away, I had stepped out from under it because I stopped focusing on Jesus and started worrying about the 'what ifs' and how I was going to be everything to everyone. The reality of the situation is that I only need to meet God's expectations.

In Mathew 14:28-31 Jesus tells Peter to step out of the boat and come to Him. Peter is focused on Jesus and he finds himself walking on water. The minute he let his fear distract him he began to sink. Peter cried out and the Lord saved him asking, "...why did you doubt?" That's what I've been doing, I've been focusing on my abilities or lack of to handle everything, which creates stress and panic because I know that I fall. I lost sight of the fact that the Lord has everything we need, He has Grace and when we focus on Him we are covered by that Grace.

I wrote the note above thinking it would help me find a bit of closure, some way to express my sorrow following the loss of my momma. I've been drowning and I'm still treading water, sometimes barely keeping my head above the surface. The difference is that even though I know the waves are still coming I also remember they are not going to take me under for good. I know that my ocean is not a bottomless pit of grief and sorrow, it is instead an endless sea of Grace and though it carries the waves of sorrow to me and allows them to wash over me, it envelopes me and protects me through this storm. "...I know, just as surely as the waves of sorrow threaten to pull me under, peace will come to calm the storm within my spirit and my grief will give way to joyful and loving memory."

       Love Always, Teresa

Teresa is a proud member of the community in New Caney, Texas. She grew up knowing that God, family, and education were the foundation of a content and successful life. Teresa is a graduate of Sam Houston State University with a degree in Political Science. She is a wife, aunt, daughter, granddaughter, niece, cousin, stand in mom, and loyal friend. Her deep and abiding faith enable her to put her whole heart into everything she does. Teresa is the co-founder of Sisson Kitchen with her husband Ronn. You can connect with her on Facebook and at www.SissonKitchen.com.

# Angela Thomas Smith

**Life after Death, my life was just being!**

Tuesday, April 1st 1975 at 5:56am I made my entrance into this world. Yes, April fool's day, the day God ordained just for me. I was born in Anderson SC to Glenn Lee and Late Catherine Martin Thomas Jr. I grew up in a very small community called Level Land in Abbeville County (17 miles south of Anderson) on Blackhill rd. One way in and one way out, only family lived on this road and we were known as the Martin's. We owed land so we raised crops and had a few pigs and chickens (I guess you could call us part time farmers). My family was rich but it wasn't much that we wanted for.

They all worked in Mills, plants and factories to provide for their families. My family exemplified the true meaning of "it takes a village to raise a child". If we misbehave whoever we were with would discipline us and then when we got home boy we got it. My mother had three kids my oldest Sister Annette who was 10 years old than me, my brother was the middle child he was 3 years older than me and I was the baby. As long as I could remember my mom and dad were separated and I spent majority of my life around my mother's family.

I accepted Christ at an early age and attended Flat Rock AME church in Anterville SC, Rev. Pope was the pastor at that time. I remember going to church every Sunday (with my Aunt

Ester Aiken) and if I didn't go I couldn't go anywhere else that day. My mom made sure we had a Christian upbringing; even if she didn't go to church we were on that green and white church bus for Sunday school, choir practice, visiting nursing homes, Vacation Bible School and every available opportunity. My great grandfather Late Rev, Murray Hunter was a pastor as well (I remember many Saturdays and Sundays going to his house, literally having church before we left there) so we had no choice but to learn the word. I loved going to church, my favorite scripture is Jeremiah 29:11(New International Version, NIV) For I know the plans I have for you," declares the Lord, "plans to prosper you and not to harm you, plans to give you hope and a future. This scripture would play an important part in my life over the years as I being this journey called Life.

Fast forward to November 1990, my mom would suddenly take ill and be in and out the hospital battling complications Lupus (a chronic, complex and prevalent autoimmune disease that affects more than 1.5 million Americans). I was 15 yrs. old at the time, my brother had gone off to SC State University so it was just my niece (Latonya who was reared in the house) and me in the home with mommy. I was a sophomore at Dixie high School in Due West, a starter on basketball team and an A/B honor roll student. My life changed drastically over the next few months. My daily schedule would consist of going to school, practice/game and back to hospital. March, 1991 my mom would call the family to hospital and she said she was tired. I remember pleading with God asking him to take me because my family needed my mom. I begged him to spare her life, she started getting better and she came home.

That Monday after Easter Sunday she would take ill again and is rushed to hospital, this time to ICU unable to talk or respond. At this time our basketball team was playing in playoff and didn't want to miss the game. I didn't want to let my team down but I knew I had to be with my mom to so my coach Dee Davis (THE BEST COACH IN THE WORLD) drove her personal vehicle to the game so that she could drop me off at hospital after the game. Dee Davis believed in me when I didn't even believe in myself. I started playing basketball because of Dee Davis in 8th grade she was my PE teacher and she saw talent in me. I never played or thought about playing before; I tried out and made the JV team. When JV season was over I was moved to varsity. This would start my love for basketball and would end of being one of the things that would cultivate my life. My freshman year I was starting and getting a lot of playing time, I really being to love playing.

I remember being dropped off at the hospital that Friday night to spend the night with my mom, still in ICU she was worst then when I left her. Still not responding, remember just sitting there watching her monitor afraid to fall asleep fearing she would leave me. I wasn't prepared for that at all. I fell off to sleep around 4:30am and few minutes into me fallen asleep I had this awful dream and it woke me. I immediately looked at the monitor and my mom had flat lined.

The nurse was calling all kind of codes and asked me to leave the room. Shortly after that nurse comes out and ask me if there was anyone I could call to come be with me. I knew that my mom was gone I could feel it all in my spirit. I just began to pray and call on the name of Jesus. I asked him to give me peace and understand if she didn't make it. I just wanted strength to make it through because I knew my family was going to take it hard. My mom was such a supportive, caring, loving and understanding person. She loved unconditional and would give you the shirt off her back. She just wanted to see everyone happy and thriving in life.

I thank God for the time I had with her she taught me so much. Days after my mom's passing I would often be reminded of something that she had shared with me over the years.

She had so many sayings she use to share with me. I remember us sitting and talking when I first became a teenager about life. She would say "treat people how you wanted to be treated not how they treat you". Luke 6:31 "Do to others as you would like them to do to you". She also would say the same people you pass on your way up you'll pass them on your back down. Don't try to be more than you are, treat people with respect from toilet cleaner to President. Remember we all are people and have feelings and we have to answer for all that we do. I don't remember crying until days after the funeral. My family coming together and us being with each other kept my mind off what was really going on. I had gotten so used to my mom being in the hospital, but realizing I was never going back to the placed I knew as home was starting to set in. My best friend at the time was also my cousin and we spent a lot of time together; we went to the same school and played basketball together. She helped me keep my mind off my mom we did everything together. I would spend days at their house, until my aunts would start complaining and trying to tell my sister how to raise me.

Oh I left out the fact that my dad didn't try to get custody of me so I ended up with my sister. My sister wasn't having all that so when opportunity presented itself for her to get out of South Carolina she was gone like the wind. I didn't want to go because I was playing basketball and was doing quite well. Didn't want to jeopardize my chance of not being able to play or get a scholarship in GA. So I stayed behind moved in with my dad's sister. My life would drastically be changing and not for the better.

Life as I knew it was over. August of 1991 I would move in with my father's sister in Anderson county SC. That would launch another journey in my life that would teach me a lot about people and family. I started a new school and met new friends many of whom I remained friends with today. Hoping and praying my dad would become more involved in my life, wrong it seemed like he drifted further away. My junior and senior year of high school would be two of the worst years of my life. Years that should've have been filled with happiness and joy. I often thought about ended my life because I felt unwanted. I fell into a deep depression, I hated being around my family because the made me feel worthless and that my life had no value. I recall hearing several family members having conversations about me that broke me. I felt like God had forgotten about me and didn't care. If it wasn't for friends in school and my involvement in sports I probably would've followed thru with those thoughts. I began to pour myself into church and got more involved in school participating volleyball, track, pageants and whatever I could to stay away from the house. Those years made me think a lot of my mom and I would cry myself to sleep, I so thankful that my mom thought enough of me when I was younger to send me to church, I had learned how to pray and call on the name of the Lord.

Around February 1993, I found out I was going to receive a scholarship to play basketball at North Greenville Jr College (North Greenville University Now), I knew that would definitely be my way out of Anderson SC. One of the most excited days of my life at that time would turn out to be the worst. No one from my family showed up for my press conference to sign and commit to attend NGC. Once again, I would get depressed and feel like no one cared, they could've even come to support me. May 1993, I would graduate, August the same year I would head off to college excited and relieved that out was out of Anderson. Fast forward I would attend NGC for one year unsure of what my future had instore for me I just knew I didn't want to return to NGC. That summer I packed and headed to Atlanta GA to live with my sister and her family.

I knew that God had a plan for me and I had to discover what it was. I got a job working at Hardees. I would work early mornings and spend my afternoon look and calling colleges trying to get in school and hopefully playing basketball. I visited Clark Atlanta and Spelman colleges; neither of them at the time was able or willing to offer me scholarship. I remember leaving a message a Morris Brown College and Coach Alvin Daniels would call me back and within days make a home visit. Long story short I step out on faith and God opened a door for me to attend Morris Brown College. Not only did I get a Scholarship; Coach Daniels would help me get a job at Papa John's pizza across the street from the school. I made some great friends that I have remained friends with even through the distance and years we stay connected.  The next three years I would play basketball and pledge a non-Greek sorority called Omega Pearl aka LOR (ladies of Royalty). I traveled to places I never traveled before; saw and experienced a lot. Made lots of mistake but learning from the mistakes is what allowed me to get where I'm at in life right now.

Not holding grudges, loving me and not allowing people to determine who I would be. I learned my self-worth. Today I'm able to share my story with others through my personal Ministry Placed with a purpose encouraging others to use their God giving gifts and talents to reach their purpose. Because God has placed us all here with a purpose and a reason. He said so in Jeremiah 29:11. Not only did he give me a personal ministry but he allowed me to move back to Anderson SC in 2009 and meet my best friend, business partner and sister Shekinah Lee Galloway.  It seems like we have known each other all our lives. We started an organization Called Pushing Grace Networking Group our mission and purpose is" building strong healthy families", one child at a time and one family at a time. I thank God that he never gave up on me.

My mom's favorite passage was Psalms 23 The LORD is my shepherd, I lack nothing.  2 He makes me lie down in green pastures, he leads me beside quiet waters, 3 he refreshes my soul. He guides me along the right paths for his name's sake.4 Even though I walk through the darkest valley, [a]I will fear no evil, for you are with me; your rod and your staff, they comfort me.⁵ You prepare a table before me in the presence of my enemies. You anoint my head with oil; my cup overflows.⁶ surely your goodness and love will follow me all the days of my life, and I will dwell in the house of the LORD forever. Someone reading this today needs to know that God is always with you, everything that we go thru we may not understand it then, but having faith and trusting that it's working for his Good. He said in his word Romans 8:28 (KJV) and we know that all things work together for good to them that love God, to them who are the called according to his purpose. Today, I challenge you to discover your purpose and what God has called you to do. He has given you a gift and he placed you here just for this time.

Before I close I want to encourage someone with a quick testimony (know you can't have a testimony if you never go thru anything, test and trials are going to come but they only come to make you stronger). Two years ago May 7th 2014, I was involved in an incident the devil was trying to take me out but God said NO, the enemy tried to kill me because he had seen what God had in store for my future. Doctors said I should not have survived, they said if I walked it would be months, but God said no! Within hours of coming out of surgery I walked. When God is for you there is no devil in hell can stop what he has ordained for you. I pray that my story will encourage you if can overcome and can to. No matter where you are in life God can turn it around. I encourage you to follow your heart and dreams. Speak life because the word says in Proverbs 18:21(KJV) Death and life are in the power of the tongue: and they that love it shall eat the fruit thereof. Be blessed and encouraged.

Closing Prayer Father God in the name of Jesus I humble myself before you right thanking you for the very person reading this book, it's no accident that they are reading this. You have ordained this before we were even created, you knew this day would come, you knew every story in this book would help someone. Father God I come against every demonic spirit that has tried to attach itself to them. I bind the spirit of fear in the name of Jesus and lose the spirit of freedom. I bind the spirit of lack and loose the spirit of overflow. I bind the spirit of suicide and homicide and loose the spirit of Life. Father God I thank you for every person that will read this and I pray their life is for every changed for your Glory. Loose your ministering Angels to speak to their spirit right now in Jesus name.

Angela Thomas Smith, I was born in Anderson SC to Late Catherine Martin Thomas and Glenn Lee Thomas Jr. I was raised in a small community called Level Land on Black bill Rd in Abbeville county SC with nothing but family. I spent most of my Adult life in Atlanta GA. I attended and play basketball at North Greenville Jr College in Tigerville, SC (now North Greenville University) and Morris Brown College in Atlanta GA. I'm the youngest of four Carolyn Annette Reynolds, Glenn Howard Groves and Quinn Germain Thomas. I'm married to Rashard M Smith. I'm Co-founder of Pushing Grace Networking Group & Community Gateway center, Founder/Ceo/Executive Director of Placed with a Purpose Ministries. My mission in life is to educate, empower and encourage individuals to be all that they can be through Christ. Jeremiah 29:11 is my favor Scripture. I love my family and my God Mother Betty Joe Lewis (this lady have been there for me from day one). Angela Thomas Smith PO Box 476 Anderson SC 29622 678-389-5700
placedwithapurpose@gmail.com

# Placida Acheru

**From Fear to Freedom**

My arrival into the Acheru family was one of great celebration and relief, wiping away the tears for an earlier lost child. My given name is Placida, which in Latin means calm, peace and serenity. My parents were both devote Christians of the Anglican church in Nigeria, a proud River State family. My father was a teacher at the time. My second name is Chukwunazam, a Nigerian word that translates to "God answers me".

My belief in God started to manifest itself around my 14th birthday. It was during a visit to my God Mother. I sat listening to a conversation between my God sister and her aunty. God came into my life that day and has not left me since. It is my belief in Him that has become the corner stone to my life and given me strength through some particularly hard times.

I was a beautiful girl, full of joy and happiness. My father particularly doted on me. He would spoil me, despite my mother's complaints, sister and two brothers that were born after me.

But all was not well. I was diagnosed with Sickle Cell Anaemia (SCA), a hereditary blood disorder, where the cells assume an abnormal, rigid, sickle-like shape under certain circumstances affecting the oxygen-carrying haemoglobin molecule in red blood cells. SCA increases a person chance of severe infections, attacks of severe pain ("sickle-cell crisis"), and stroke, and there is also an increased risk of death (50% affected die before aged 50). Sickle-cell disease occurs when a person inherits two abnormal copies of the haemoglobin gene, one from each parent.

SCA was only becoming understood in the 1950's and there was little knowledge of its implications for an individual. Approximately 300,000 people are dialogised each year in the African Sub-continent. For me, SCA means constantly inconsistent feelings of lethargy, tiredness and breathlessness, and even severe pain for days and months that can put me in hospital requiring a blood transfusion. It dominated my life growing up. Although, all my family and friends wanted to help and protect me, the result was I felt smothered with love. I wanted independence from SCA. I did not want it to define me or my relationships with people. I wanted a normal life.

Every day of my life, as I faced this health challenge that made me alternate between good and bad days, my family, doctors and even the community told me what I could not do or rather, they did not want me to do, fearing another sickle-cell crisis. My resolve helped me break from the emotional strangle hold and gave me stability. I was determined to live a normal life.

Determination can only go so far. I wanted love. I wanted a partner in life. I saw all my friends in relationships and my belief in the Gospel intensified this desire for a loving partner and children of my own.

The reality was very different. Everyone that I met and fell in love with me wanted the same as me, a long loving relationship. Fear and uncertainty scared partners away. As soon as SCA was mentioned I would hear the same response …. "I love you, but" … then more heartache.

One day, in my early 30s I thought I had found that man. The man with enough love and courage to take not only me, but my SCA into his heart and live with whatever life throws at us. It was going to be the wedding of the century. I was so happy. Everyone around me knew how much I had wanted this day. My Dad was going to make sure this was going to be a very special day. He loved me so much.

1000 invitations were sent out. My father even announced the marriage on the radio. I was well known from my participation in my local Pentecostal church and far more than the 1,000 invitees attended to celebrate the grand event. God had answered my prayers. My life was complete.

Three months later I was fighting to save my marriage and wondering what I had done wrong. I was one who never questioned God. The realities of my SCA started to create strains in my marriage, amplified by my husband's family. Prejudice and doubts about me being able to produce healthy children started to pull him away from me. The severe heartbreak I was feeling was becoming unbearable. Deep in my spirit, I felt God did not ever want me to be happy. Why would He steal my joy? What did I ever do to anyone to deserve this? The whole situation was killing me inside. I could not express my pain with anyone. I had trained myself to bear the pain of SCA and hide it from the people around me. I did not want anyone to see me crying from the daily pain. The same protection system pulled the pain of my failed marriage inside too, even though the pain was far worse than SCA could ever inflict on me.

For two years, I carried the hurt and refused to accept my marriage was over even though my husband had disappeared. I had no idea where my husband was living. His family had taken him from me and changed his name, making sure that I could never fine him again. Eventually, though I found him and tried for another 2 years to see if I could restore my marriage. I believed deep in my heart, he loved me, but was not strong enough to follow his heart. He just needed to believe me and get passed what he had been told, "she is a sick woman and she would die".

Seven years passed, after this time I realised that I had to face the reality that my dream of a happy normal marriage and life with my husband were over. I could not stay in Nigeria. If I was to get passed this everything had to change. This was a big decision. When you have a life threatened disease like SCA, you have systems and protection all around you to help you deal with the unpredictable changes in your health.

I had always liked the idea of living in London. I had a Master's Degree in Guidance and Counselling and a good job at a Nigerian College. I needed a 'fresh start'. I left the safety of the environment I had known for the last 37 years and headed to London with all my savings.

London is much more expensive than Nigeria. My savings vanished within months. The streets may be paved with gold for some, but you have to work hard to access it. I do not know if Coaching found me or I found Coaching, but the skills I had learnt to cope with SCA and my life's heartbreaks helped people I spoke too. I decided to make this my career. I used the last of my savings to buy a laptop and started to learn about social media. I was going to take the lessons I had learnt and teach others how to cope with the problems in their lives. I wanted to help people and people found what I had to say did really help them.

I launched Coaching 4 Excellence, my online mentoring business. I started to feel more confident as I started to help people. I started feeling value in myself and my confidence increased. It took a huge effort and often my SCA would set me back. I refused to let it beat me.

In promoting my business, my online presence started to increase my audience. I began receiving invitations to radio and television shows. On a particular television program, everything changed. I consented to an interview in which the host encouraged me to tell the story of my break up. I use to avoid talking about the heartache caused by my failed marriage. I felt it was me that had failed and I did not want to acknowledge doubt in myself. I knew it was not me. It was my husband's love not being strong enough, but I could not let it leave my mind. The interview was the cognitive therapy I needed. The pain in my heart left as I forgave everyone and I forgave myself. I said sorry to God for blaming Him too.

As my business grows, I help more and more people face the pain that holds them back from realising their potential. I believe that I have improved the lives of thousands worldwide to systematically transform and create wealth in their lives.

The emotional torments, struggles with a low self-esteem and lack of money have pushed me to the edge, where total failure and collapse into a black hole seemed a real reality. I have learned that an essential key to life is to trust, do not keep your pain locked inside and keep your resolve. Believe in yourself.

It took a little while, but I have escaped a series of bedsits and after volunteering for Crisis at Christmas an organization that supports the homeless, found a man that loves me and my SCA. God had a plan, It's all very clear to me. I have a story to share and help others transform their lives. The fear and pain may seem like they will never go away, remember "It Shall Come to Pass" My husband and I now live in a very comfortable penthouse apartment in South East London that overlooks the Thames River. My business continues to grow, reinventing itself every day as I grow with it. You never know with life, but I am thankful for everything that has ever happened, and I pray that happiness and health will stay with me for the rest of my days.

Placida Acheru is one of UK's top business accelerators, mentor and brand visibility strategist. Founder of Coaching4Excellence and Unleashed Women's Network. She is dedicated to guiding others toward taking charge of their lives, breaking through roadblocks to systematically transform their everyday into the power to create wealth.

This extremely determined and driven individual is empowering women across the globe to be independent, gifting them the knowledge and passion to transform their lives. Overcoming her own personal obstacles such as growing up in Nigeria with sickle cell anaemia, allows Placida to use her own story in training programs to create motivation and encourage others, with full attendance at her seminars. Her social media reach is now in excess of 100,000 and recently Placida launched her own online magazine- Her Inspiration, reaching 680,000 in its first week.

Placida shows her clients how to properly apply successful business fundamentals of running a company from Planning, Mapping, and Financial strategies to gaining the motivation to push forward. When working with her, one acquires offline and online marketing strategies, discovering and maximizing the opportunities that come their way.

She is a straight talking Business Coach who helps clients get laser focused on their goals.

Placida has been featured in digital prints (People.co.uk), TV shows (Sky 182 Ben TV, OH TV, The Sporah Show) She's also on the list of Top 100 Most Influential Black People on digital/social media drawn by eelanmedia.com

She is also a radio host, Keep Your Dream Alive Radio featured on Itunes.

"Placida is one of those rare people that are top notch in all she does. She has drive, dedication to learning, and is passionate about sharing her wisdom with other entrepreneurs. As a Diamond Member of her Mastermind group, I am impressed with her attention to detail, her organization and business vision. She is a mentor to me in many ways. When I am discouraged or confused about a strategy, she always aids me in getting **out of my confusion** and I am encouraged by her belief in my abilities and that leads me to be bold and my best. I respect her as a conscientious business woman and highly recommend her as a coach" ~ - Jane Morrison: Executive Coach- Reinventing your Career

"Placida is one of the most captivating coaches/presenters I have had the privilege of experiencing. Her eternal optimism is underpinned by a fabulous sense of humour/humanity against compelling business acumen. She is a strong networker and great asset to any forum she graces with her presence." - Marie Augustin - Education Management Professional

"Placida is an excellent coach that drives her clients to perform beyond even their own expectations. She delivers real results. When it comes to social media branding, you don't need to look anywhere else. An accomplished public speaker and event organizer, she's the ideal professional partner for any business owner and executive looking to move to the next level." ~ Saheed Adegbite - Director, Budget and Organizational Development at International Fund for Agricultural Development

"I met Placida when she organised and hosted a special meeting in London for organisers of groups hosted on meetup.com. She introduced us to Scott Heiferman, the CEO of meetup.com. Her professional and personable presentation motivated me to attend further meetings and seminars run by her which proved very valuable." Frankie Sinclair- Web Content Manager at Royal Mail

Event and website links
1. http://placidaacheru.com
2. http://coaching4excellence.com
3. http//unleashedwomensnetwork.com
4. http://placidaacheru.com/visionactivation
5. http://womanunleashyourpotential.com

# Deborah Stevens

**BATTLE TEARS....TO SAVE A ROSE**

My hopes in writing this book is that each person that reads it can find a connection to these events; although different would spark a memory of a personal battle they have won. There are bits and pieces of my childhood I remember vaguely; and some that stick in my brain. I do remember my Great Grandmother who cried daily about dying. At the time I was not a Christian but a practicing Catholic. I would receive all of my sacraments and would continue to live the Catholic life into my adulthood. My memories of death and heaven was that why wouldn't that be a good thing. Being raised Catholic and receiving all of the sacraments I saw Heaven as a wonderful place of joy and love.

My Mother who became my soul mate through life always struggled to keep me close to God. She made sure that I had nice clothing to wear to church and that I attended Sunday school and was always included in all church activities. She was as I know someone who never lost faith even with challenges that she faced. She became a widow at 24 years old and led a life of shock treatments and mental illness, and was always labeled the Crazy one. She always showed her love of everything that God created and she loved me with all of her being.

In my Portuguese and Irish family all of the women helped to raise the grandchildren, children and great-grandchildren.

We were all cousins and sisters and brothers too. My great-grandmother would make kale soup and store it in the back hall and it was delicious. Some of the Portuguese cooking I inherited and also the Irish temper.

One of my fondest memories as a child was when my great-grandfather who we called Vu-Vu would take me to his friends and I would sing" I am Debbi Dawson and I'm here to bring you ale a lager beer." Some people today would feel that it was the exploitation of a child but I knew that it wasn't. He was just so proud of my singing talents. I would also get my tap shoes and dance for him he thought that the sun rose and set on me, I miss him so much.

My grand-mother took care of me and raised me because Mom had been ill and hospitalized several times. My Mom had 18 nervous breakdowns before her mid-twenties. She always had that smile and she loved children. That is why today I find myself teaching Sunday school because of her. I feel that she leads me to take care and protect and teach the children something she placed in my heart; besides I get great joy from doing this.

One day I remember that everyone said that I was ill. I guess I lost a great deal of weight because I had as they called it that time trench mouth. I had been playing a great deal in the dirt and had gotten an infection in my mouth. I played inside one day and almost fell out a window. I was a very active child but fragile when it came to getting cuts, scrapes and stitches. One day was calling up for mom she was always called her Rosie, she wanted to know where our new found kittens had gone.

My mom yelled down to her that she had seen them with my Great-grandmother and she felt that they had been disposed of. Such a sad day in the house a happiness of our cat Hazel who had a litter of kittens and after they were born they were disposed of. We as children didn't like it when our pets were taken away so we never grew to love our newest pets.

My VuVu passed away in the home, but I wasn't able to tell him goodbye and that I would miss him. My cousin Johnny and I were upstairs getting our baths and ready for bed when I heard strange things happening downstairs, a really weird feeling was in the middle of my stomach but being 3 years old I didn't know what it meant; that was the last time I would get to have my Great Grand Father near. I feel that it affected me at that time that I remembered the rest of my life. Around that time, I experienced my first physical abuse. My Grandmothers boyfriend use to watch me when she went to work; When I described what he did to me; the police were called and he was taken away briefly. My Grandmother had gone to the Police station and told them that I was lying and it never happened; it must have worked because he returned to the house. That was the last day that I would see my Grandmother, years later if would affect our relationship forever. I had lost most of my faith in people and especially her.

A few years later would come the bed wetting the sleep walking and the visits. By visits I mean was people that would come and protect me from the boogie man so to speak. That is also when I sunk into deep depression; and at 7, I started to think of suicide. During those years my Dad also asked me to stay home from school while he worked to watch my Mom. She was going through another breakdown and he needs me to be there to keep her from doing it. I remember one day I called out to GOD and told him I want to go to school to see my friends and that he needed to take Mommy and put her where people could help her. That next day I was calling 911 and the fire department had to come and retrieve her from the roof of the apartment building we live in; at 7 that stays in your mind forever.

 I had a friend that I made in the building her name was Hazel and she would have me in for her special homemade tomato soup that was so good but the company and conversations

we shared I cherished. Now that I recall it there were several angels in my life; I believe she was one.
During most of my childhood and adolescents my Mom was in the hospital. I remember when a family member would come into my room they would tell me that she will be home soon but she needs the rest. I would stare at her picture and cry for hours; I missed my Mom so much. But I never thought that GOD loved me I didn't know who he was. I just went to church and loved Jesus and new that he was there, I always thought he was punishing me for some reason.

But when a woman gets older and meets a man their own age they are allowed to reach into their adolescents and bring that time back to where they felt the butterflies in their stomachs and feel like a schoolgirl in love. I think that is how it should be there is too much focus on getting old and trying to stay young that we miss all the things that we possess at that time. How could love be so blind as to fool you into thinking that you are really in love with someone you meet rather than the unexplained emotion? How could all of this lead us into blindness and we are willing to risk everything. Could that be the reason why one spends countless hours looking for something and find themselves in the process? Do we lead our emotions to the extent to where we would lose not only everything but our identities as well?

**Everything I do; I do for you:**
**I never thought that one could live with a broken heart,**
**To not get peace from birds that sing,**
**To miss someone so much the pain is intense,**
**To continue to look for you in every face,**
**To tell you I love you each day and night,**
**To seek your guidance and look for signs,**
**To feel the loneliness, to be consumed,**
**To lift my head each day and smile,**
**Forcing myself to be kind with optimism,**
**The search for your Mom will never end,**
**Until we meet and can share love again.**

These words ring true for the feelings that I had when I lost the most important person in my life; my Mom. I thought each day would be easy and never could bring myself to think of life without her. She was the only positive thing in my life and now I can really appreciate how much she brought to my life now that she is gone.

During all of my years of abuse I always felt that God had placed this as a punishment. My Mom suffered for so many years since her husband died and she became a single Mom left with no money and a child to raise. She not only was a single parent and again; but one who would battle several years of mental illness. When she was diagnosed with Stage 4 lung cancer she refused treatment she later told me she wanted to be with Daddy. I looked at her with tears streaming down my face; held her hand and smiled.

Today I am still trying to find the way to forgive people who have abused me; it is a long process. I am beginning to find that peace. I am learning to find true peace; love for myself and the courage to always see a clear and brighter future. Fear does not grip me anymore I embrace and claim victory most days.  I am not perfect but I trust the one who is.

I am finding that my faith is always there and God has placed everyday angels into my life to love encourage and to help me to see who I really am.  A strong woman who has come to grow and enjoy life no matter what challenges it may bring. Deborah Hegre; a native New Englander would write short stories and poems when she was a young woman. She shared her stories with her Aunt Vivian who was an avid reader. Vivian told her that she should always continue to write and pursue her dreams.

Deborah always saw herself as a doer and a dreamer. She was born poor; she saw her family struggle and she knew she could do more and wanted more. Deborah loved to read her reading was the old literature.

Deborah focused on education and planned on continuing her education. At 16 she had to drop out of school and help her widowed Mother support the family.
Deborah struggled sometimes with the need to have and the need to dream for what she wanted. She worked for several years in factories where she was paid to work and not to think. Deborah kept her dreams close and didn't care about what others said.

In 1977 Deborah acquired her GED; a major accomplishment for her. Later when she married she went back to school to learn a trade but she always managed to add a creative writing course.

Deborah was famous for carrying small notebooks wherever she went. She would always expect to find a situation to write about. Life is interesting and we must be aware of the finer things that we take for granted.

Deborah wished that someday she could be a great writer. She did some illustrations for children's books but soon lost interest. Deborah would read the great books; classics and dream about visiting all over the world to write.
In 2013 at Eastern Connecticut State College was of the assignments that she had was to write a business plan for the Willimantic Victorian Association. She met the Head of the Association and after several weeks of research and execution her and her team received honorable mention and their business plan was chosen.

Deborah has worked as a caregiver and an advocate for individuals of disabilities. She has worked with adolescents with traumatic disorders and individuals with Brain Injuries. Deborah continues to write her passion and to help others overcome any challenges or abuse they have overcome. She continues to work with women who want to become entrepreneurs and to work a home based business.

# Katrina M. Walker

**Beauty in Brokenness**

It takes time to put things together, even when they are not broken. The amount of time it takes to put things back together again after things have been shattered takes even more time. The devastation of brokenness is hard to bounce back from. My brokenness happened without warning. I was at a lost with time and years spent loving a person I believed loved me back. Have you ever broken your favorite vase, artifact or necklace? If you have, then you would know that many times the pain is real. Let's take it a step further, have you ever had a broken relationship that takes time to heal from? The amount of time it takes to heal from the torment of loss is lengthy. Love is tricky sometimes is what I was told. My Love life had pretty much been a sum of disappointments. I was a woman looking for love in many places.

I have been on many roller-coasters in my emotions while dealing with men. One man in particular was a catalyst for me to grow into the freedom that I know now. He was the man I thought I wanted to marry. He was the man that I loved with all my heart and that I had committed myself. It was a fairy-tale that had seemed to fall into my lap, well, at least I believed that he was good for me. He was committed to me daily and on every effort, he made me happy. He was the "one" until one day he left everything, including me without an excuse. There was no trace of where he had gone or why. He just never came back home. It would be weeks before I could hear about his whereabouts. It was definitely a shattered piece for me. I later discovered that he was still a married man.

Yes, I discovered he was married, he never told me and of course I never heard from him on the matter. For years I had dated him and not seen a trace of him being married or even dating anyone else besides me. It was clear afterwards that I had ignored simple warning signs that I had deemed normal before he disappeared. I was troubled by his absence to the point of depression but the Lord delivered me out of the situation and helped me to overcome all that I was faced with in that season of my life.

Finding out that I was dating a married man for me was the lowest point in my life. All things happen for a reason. I believe the Lord was releasing me from even more hurt down the line because the break-up happened suddenly. Before the break-up, things were perfect. When I say perfect, I mean perfect. Had I married him I would have truly been in deeper emotional bondage and struggled even harder to get over the failure of the relationship.

We were like a family. We did everything together. I was under the impression that he was a divorced man that had a bad break-up with his "previous" wife. I was extremely supportive of all he desired to do and he was supportive of me as well. We had dated for a long time and we even were planning a wedding. He was pressuring me to marry him as well, he wanted to push up the wedding date to make things happen faster and to be a "family" he said. I was dating a man with goals and dreams. I was dating a man that I thought loved the Lord more than he loved me! We would go to church weekly together.

My family adored him and everyone had helped to make our big day happen. My mother believed he was an awesome man that would make me happy. That she had finally found a son-in-law that would treat me with respect and love. He made me happy because he was gentle, kind, and compassionate.

Although most people loved him, I had a few relatives that felt that I could do better, one great aunt in particular was always there to pray and offer guidance throughout the relationship. I will forever be grateful for her wisdom and love.

I contribute part of my personal freedom from this relationship to her prayers. There is power in having someone with more wisdom praying for you. She was a member of the body of Christ, God used her to bring about his will in my life. I came out stronger than when I went into the relationship, this is the benefit that I received from older and mature women praying offered me. Through much prayer and support I gained my strength back and came back even stronger. After he left, I was so depressed that I lost my job a week later. I had to search out what happened because he did not contact me after that day I last saw him.

After contacting some of his relatives, I would find out that he was still married to his wife and had a family. Not only did I find out that he was married but that on numerous occasions he had taken advantage of women in the same way that he had done to me. He would often stay with women for long periods of times and then leave them without explanation. This was a cycle that he resorted to avoid his own issues and responsibilities with life. Often times when a person is displeased with life, they will begin to create a false life to help them cope with the reality that they have not measured up to their own predicted successes.

In hind sight I saw and noticed that he would avoid responsibility. After talking to his relatives and counselors, I came to the conclusion that I had to move up in faith. During the time after the break-up, I developed an even stronger prayer life. The break-up also impacted my daughter as well as me, it had a huge impact on my daughter's relationships with men. He left an imprint on her life for all eternity, to this very day, she says that she is afraid to love whole-heartedly because of him leaving unexpectedly. After all, that she endured with me, she has gone on to become very successful as a college graduate. Due to all of the trauma that transpired from that relationship, I am still overcoming in the area of relationships. I have developed many ways to identify how to know the person you are getting involved with. I developed an even closer relationship with the Lord, I felt like breaking up with him put me back on track to my spiritual walk. A huge indication that a person is for you, is how you develop spiritually.

If the person begins to block your spiritually then you are more than likely not in God's will. My great aunt's prayers were answered and I would develop an even more advanced walk with God. Often times, there is beauty in brokenness. If you never know pain, then you will never experience the fullness of joy. The bible says that weeping may endure for a night but joy comes in the morning. Brokenness is like night, sooner or later it has an end.

The beauty in him leaving me far outweighed the amount of grief I felt for that amount of time. At times I think of him for a second! Then reality says, when something is not for you, it just is not for you. We have to learn to take the good of our brokenness and recognize that out of it comes wisdom, knowledge, and power. When something is broken, we want to throw it out, maybe it's a necklace or vase. However, when you value something, you don't cast it away with ease. I believe that brokenness is like that. Just because an experience is painful and emotionally draining, do not cast it away. God allowed it to happen, he wants you to remember it. He wants you to learn from it, grow from it and build on it. This is the beauty in brokenness.

Although I experienced abandonment, rejection and hurt, I had to learn that there was beauty in what I went through. I learned that I could fix myself, with counseling, I could repair myself with the Lord's help. There was beauty in leaning on God. There was beauty in trusting God. There was beauty in being free from possible further danger. I learned to keep broken pieces and put them back together again. I was blessed by my brokenness. Out of brokenness I came out with greater joy. After he left me I thought that my world was crumbling but through prayer, perseverance, and strength, I rose above my own fear of failure. I worked multiple jobs to be sure that my family was properly taken care of, I trusted God and he showed me favor.

If you are suffering with brokenness, I pray that you find beauty in brokenness. There is hope for those that are broken by abandonment, fear, hurt, rejection. There is hope because God makes all things beautiful in his timing. I pray that your ashes, your broken pieces and your sorrows are turned into beauty. I pray that you will get up out of your rumble and make a decision to live, love, and thrive because God will grant you favor when you trust him!

Katrina M. Walker is an IT Professional, Semi-Professional Soccer player and the proud Mother of one daughter, Kyna Boyd who is currently working on her Master's Degree in Architecture.

https://www./katrinawalkerfrombrokentounbreakable.wordpress.com

 kwalker1127@gmail.com

# Tina Garner

**Our infinite love**

Back in the summer 1978, I met this guy named Ricky Garner. I still remember that day like it was yesterday, I was at a friend's house sitting in the back of a goodtime van listening to music. Here came this guy and introduced himself to me. I was very shy I said hello and told him my name. Ricky later had told me he had feel in love with me as soon as he laid eyes on me. I soon fell for him too.
August of 1979 I had gone to my dad's in midland Texas for a couple of weeks the longest 2 weeks ever. I cried and couldn't breathe missing Ricky so much. I was definitely in love. As soon I came back home I ended up pregnant.

 We wanted to get married right away. We went to get our marriage license in Kaufman County. My mom had to sign for me to get married I was only 15 and Ricky was 19.
The wedding was at our preacher's home and performed by Bro. Thorton. On Our wedding night of January 18, 1980 we ate at sonic for $7.00 on the house to congratulate us also I was a car hop there. We didn't tell anyone where we ate that night till our first Anniversary. That was our secret. our honeymoon was staying the night in our first apartment.

The next day was our wedding shower at my mom's house. I already had a lot of things for the apartment a bed, tv, dresser, towels, pots and pans. Ricky only had car and a Laundry basket of stuff. I was 15 and naive and pregnant. I could not wait to take care of my little baby boy spoil and love him and put clothes on him like a baby doll. Lil rick was born June 20, 1980 of course he was named after his dad. my second child Aaron Blake it was a fun pregnancy I had only gain 25 pounds and felt good.

Here came the third child Krista Ann I had a lot of back pain with her and ate lots of sweets also till this day I love sweets. My boys grow up playing football, baseball, basketball, bike races, motorcycle racing my daughter ballet, dance, cheer, basketball, drill team and she even had her own motorcycle.

We moved from the city to the country bought 10 acres for the kids to ride their motorcycles. I didn't know what my husband had got me into, the grass was to my knees the house wasn't even livable. He told me to look past the ugly and see what it could be and I did. So we worked on the house and in the yard that's what we did. we loved our little home.

2004, I was in a car wreck I was coming back from taking my son to get fitted for his tux for prom. I dropped him back off at school and I was coming home to go to work when I saw a bulldozer on a trailer head right at my 2001 mustang. God was with me, in my mind's eye I thought if I swerve and I would get hit a little or not at all. paramedics had to care flight me to parkland.

The guy that seen what happen, knew it was me and went to the school to tell my son. My son did know his dad's new number so they had to go back to the tux place to get the number. My son had Remembered that I have gave it to the lady. Then they called my husband and told him a bulldozer fell on my car, all he could think about was that disc jockey that had died when a bulldozer fell over the bridge and landed on his car killing the disc jockey.

My husband was scared to death for me, even my son rick I remember waking up in the hospital and seeing the look on his face he was scared for his momma. My husband stayed by my side the whole time day and night helped do whatever he needed to do for me. He showed me his love thru sickness and health.

Ricky would take me out every Friday and Saturday night to eat, the movies or to the bar to dance, the casino to gamble or play Texas Hold'em or to get a scratch ticket at the local store or just riding on our Harley it was like we were the only two people on the road. We enjoyed each other and had a lot of fun together.

Then in 2014 Ricky had a heart attack 100% blockage he should have not made it but he did. At that time, I was not ready for God to take him from me. That was my worst fear if I ever lost my husband.

How would I take care of myself or support myself? I never really had to work Ricky had always took care of me and spoiled me through the years. It was so scary to me I couldn't even imagine my life without him.

So God gave us another year to be together and prepare me for what was about to come. The morning of April 15, 2016 my worst fear became my reality. my husband was killed in head on collision on his motorcycle.

 He was my soulmate, my husband of 36 years, my best friend, my provider and my security he was my whole world. He was a Great man, my children's dad, my grandson's grandpa. Ricky's love was as endless as the stars. We showed our love to each other every day. We would have called each other and text every day I love you or I love you more. I can still think of him and he still puts a smile on my face every day.

The past four months has been a journey I have a blank page to write a new chapter in my life. To be on my own and the person I was meant to be for Gods Glory. Since that day I wake up each morning and live my life. To write about from fear to freedom. How God has brought me though this far is amazing to tell.

My husband knew before he died I was writing a chapter in a book he said you better get to writing that it was my time to make my dreams come true.
I know he is in a better place I wouldn't wish him back. through our infinite love, a lifetime of memories and our kids, family and the selfies we took. Listening to our favorite songs and seeing red cardinals. I keep him alive always in my heart. Thank you Ricky for showing me your love that is never ending.

I'm 52yrs old and a recently widowed, I was a wife of 36 years, a Mother of three Amazing Children, a Grandma of one Awesome Grandson, I've been teaching skincare classes for about 7 years now. My journey is to empower women to believe in herself, feel Beautiful inside and out and succeed in life.

# **Phyllis Turner**

**Fatherless to Fearless**
**Dads, Daughters, Duty**

I was born in Lynwood, California, joining an already dysfunctional family of 9. My brother Stephen would be born in two more years and complete our family of 10.
When I was 3 years old, my father walked out the door and never returned. I never saw or heard from him again. Mom only spoke of him when I asked questions and even then, I got conflicting answers throughout my life. My father was one of 6 men that fathered mom's 10 kids. My brother Daniel is my only full sibling but none of us ever saw each other as "step-brothers and sisters" ever. We were always just one, big, seriously dysfunctional family.

When I started kindergarten. To say I was terrified and shy was an understatement. I didn't want to go to school and be without my siblings or my mom. I sat in the back of the room at a round table, all by myself and barely spoke to anyone. I did make a few friends somehow but I'm sure I was considered weird by most of my classmates. I wonder if being born #9 had anything to do with me being so shy? Nobody asked for my opinion and I'm sure I didn't have much of a say when it came to making decisions at home. This is also one of the places where my feelings and thoughts of being "insignificant" came from.

A pretty scary memory from right around that same time was when Stephen and I were sleeping on our bed in the dining room and being awoken by red lights flashing on the wall beside our bed. There were paramedics in the house and I just remember feeling the high-tension and being told not to move from the bed. It turns out, two of my older brothers (J.C. & "Bubba") were sharing a room at the front of the house and Bubba had slit his wrist and there was blood all over the bed and the floor of their room.

There was a post office just down the street. My two older brothers were in high school and often times would babysit the rest of us while mom went out carousing. I remember driving around at night one time and being afraid my mom would find out and we'd all get in trouble.

J.C. had a motorcycle and would give us rides on it around the yard. I don't remember going on the road on it at this point but I do remember burning my leg pretty bad on the muffler...mom wasn't home and he was so upset! I remember him putting butter on it because that's what people did back then but learning later it was probably the worst thing he could have put on it. This house also had an old outhouse in the backyard and a separate house in the way-back that my two older brothers later moved into. Around the time I was in second grade, the family at home was down to Stephen, me, Daniel and David.

Mom was going through a tough time (I'm not sure if it was alcohol or prescription drugs) but the 4 of us were sent to various foster homes. None of us were together in the same home. We got shuffled around a few times and I finally settled in with the Stauffers. There was a teenage daughter that they were in the process of adopting and another girl about my same age. I started school there and I remember going camping, and Ms. Stauffer making dresses for the other little girl and me. She also made us awesome Easter baskets so I'm guessing I was there for close to a year. I truly have no

idea. I was able to have visits with my mom occasionally after a while before we were all back home again.
I don't have a lot of memories from then till about 6th grade. Probably due to my mom's problems, I lived with my sister Linda, her husband Joe and their son Michael during my 6th grade school year.

I claimed my first "boyfriend" during that year. To say I idolized my sister Linda would be an understatement. She was drop-dead gorgeous and I wanted to be just like her. Her husband was very handsome, caring, compassionate and fun. They seemed to have it all together. She was a nurse and I loved watching her get ready for the day…she used hot rollers in her hair all the time. I don't remember her ever looking unkempt. She always polished her nails and had her hair and makeup done.

Today, Linda suffers from paranoid schizophrenia and none of us know where she is.

I also lived with my sister Peggy and her husband off and on. I think she took me in whenever mom was having a hard time with my brothers. They were all pretty mischievous. Peggy is the first born in the family so she was actually more like a mother figure to me than a sibling. Peggy started having kids when I was around 12, so I was the perfect babysitting age. I loved her kids as if they were my own. I learned so much from hanging out and caring for them. I'm sure that if it were not for my older sisters, I would not be where I am today.

I had my first kiss when I was in 8th grade with a short-lived relationship and lost my virginity when I was 16. I never even knew saying "no" was an option. My mother never talked to me about sex. This boyfriend was pretty controlling. He always had to know where I was, who I was with and even picked out my swimsuits. He didn't want other guys to see my body so I wore something like a tankini even though I worked hard to stay fit. I ended up dating this guy for 3 years and we broke up when he got tired of me being friendly and flirtatious with too many guys at school and at work. Sometimes it was friendly and flirtatious but sometimes it was much more than that. This would become my pattern.

I attended college for a year and spent that year picking attractive boys out at a party and making it my goal for the evening to sleep with them. I always won. Or so I thought. Needless to say, my marriage has been wrought with heartache due to my insatiable hunger for male attention. I thank God above that for whatever reason, my husband has stood by me, regardless, and still loves me after everything I've put him through.

I have spent the last 3 years in counseling and therapy working on myself and trying to uncover the reasons for my patterns of behavior that has caused so much pain in our marriage and I believe it all boils down to not knowing my father as I was growing up.

Being fatherless can cause a girl to grow up feeling abandoned, unlovable, insignificant, not worthy of a man's love and lacking self-confidence. Low self-esteem, poor self-image, avoiding engaging her emotions, yet, always feeling a void in her soul. I've always been very insecure, carried a lot of hurt and resentment around and needed validation from the males in my life.

 Even those I didn't know. I subconsciously did things to sabotage my marriage thinking that he was probably going to leave me at some point anyhow, so why go through the charade? Just get to it and get it over with.

My portrait of a loving relationship between a man and a woman had been severely distorted. My mother was married several times and men were always in and out of our house so that's what I learned was "normal."

So, how did I overcome these issues? It started when I forgave my father for several things.
- I forgave him for walking out on us and leaving my mom with 9 kids to raise on her own, which was impossible.
- I forgave him for leaving me without the foundation I needed to develop a healthy level of confidence, self-esteem and a positive self-image.
- I forgave him for leaving me and not protecting me.
- I forgave him for not loving ME enough to stick around.

I realize now, that my father probably had his own set of baggage from his own childhood that he had to deal with and also, that it's very possible my mother asked him to leave. So, how can I hold it against him?

One of the hardest lessons I've had to learn over the years is how to love unconditionally. Not just loving the people in my life unconditionally, but what I overlooked for so many years is the importance of loving myself along with everyone else. For the longest time, because of my father, I didn't see myself as lovable or worthy of unconditional love from anybody. But, as I've peeled back the layers of this onion and like stripping layers upon layers of paint off of a piece of antique furniture, I'm finding myself restored to my original beauty. Not physical beauty per se, but internal beauty, and I love who I am.

I'm not that little girl whose own flesh and blood walked out the door and never returned. I'm not that little girl who waited for daddy to come home from work day after day after day. I'm not that little girl who grew to understand that daddy must not have loved me enough for some reason. As the years came and went, I learned that I wasn't loveable to anyone. If my own father couldn't love me...how would anyone else?

Self-love is mainly a matter of unconditional self-acceptance, with a bit of appreciation and compassion for oneself tossed in for good measure. Learning to accepting myself unconditionally without having to meet certain criteria or fulfill certain conditions was a tough lesson to learn and I'm still learning! In other words, not giving myself impossible standards to live up to.

*Conditions like:*

- I have to be successful.
- I have to be thin and pretty.
- I have to be giving of myself all of the time.
- I have to be constantly productive.
- I have to earn a certain level of income.

This list can go on and on. Setting conditions for ourselves to try to live up to is setting ourselves up for failure and depression. Even if we manage to meet some of them, we will never meet them all and we will constantly be beating ourselves up, and for what?

Forgiveness and getting rid of the conditions and constantly affirming my worth on an ongoing basis is what caused my world to change from the inside out.

Finally forgiving my father and then learning to love myself unconditionally has been the key to my overcoming my damning behaviors and thoughts. Today, I am no longer the sad, depressed, love-hungry girl that I have been my entire life. Today, I am me and I am not just "good enough" but I'm boundless! I'm FEARLESS!

Phyllis I Turner is a freelance writer, columnist & photographer who enjoys non-fiction writing on a myriad of topics. She has garnered most of her experience through creative writing on her blogs, guest blogging, writing for magazines, website copy, and training manuals. She is no

stranger to marketing via social media with active accounts on Facebook, Instagram, Twitter, Pinterest & LinkedIn. Writing since her pre-teenage years, Phyllis has always had a passion for writing and traveling. She is a writer with the heart of a gypsy, a wife, mother of one, Vero Beach Florida beach bum, lover of food, animals, sunsets and all things outdoors. She lives in Vero Beach, FL with her husband Jon. Visit her website at:
Www.cheekychickscafe.com

# Shirley La Tour

**FREE: Are you THERE yet?**

What is fear? Google defines it as an unpleasant emotion caused by the belief that someone or something is dangerous, likely to cause pain, or a threat. There is both healthy and unhealthy fear but I will be referring to unhealthy fear.
We have all heard the phrase "beauty is in the eye of the beholder" well I'm here to tell you so is fear. What may not consume one may devour another even to the point of depression or suicide. This fear can be from your upbringing, fear of what others think, fear of where to go next, fear of whether to leave or whether to stay in an unfulfilled marriage, fear of rejection, fear of failure, or even fear of succeeding. Fear robs of joy, peace, happiness, strength. It slowly kills like a viper, sucks out life and leads to DEATH: spiritual death, mental and emotional death, and finally if not turned around, physical death

. Fear keeps us from our God appointment and the anointing placed over our lives. How do I know? I'm so glad you asked! I walked through this fear for well over 10 years. Growing up in a home with domestic violence and male dominance led me to believe that some behaviors were "normal" when in reality it was anything but what God had designed from the beginning of the world. This view was further tainted by the fact that my parents were in ministry, pastors in fact. I was brought up in church and gave my life to Christ at the age of 12. I knew the scriptures, saw many miracles, signs and wonders, demons cast out but home life did not match what was being taught. This learned behavior can and did carry over to my adulthood. After 24 years of an unfulfilled, ungodly "Christian" marriage, my parents divorced. Of six children I am still the only sibling who has said "I do." I sometimes wonder why but I know God has a different purpose for my life. Without some specific obstacles, I could not progress or experience the great things He has in store for my life. Let the saga begin!

October 25, 2014 is a day I will always remember. First allow me to set the stage for you: Life was going as usual; home, husband and children, Pastor's Wife, full time Army Soldier/Registered Nurse, part time home business, volunteer nurse in the community, networker. Busy life right? I went to a networking breakfast where a lady from Houston was the guest speaker. I had seen her on a TV show once but of course we had never met. I knew her story but she did not know mine.

We were in a casual setting at a restaurant in Killeen, Texas. Gathered around long rectangular tables, I sat to the right of her across the table. As she began to talk to the group of women there, I noticed she kept looking at me. All of a sudden she stopped in the middle of her sentence and looked straight at me. I was paying attention to her wisdom for the group so when she turned to me directly and stopped, it kind of startled me.

Her words to me: "I know you don't know me but I must be obedient. I do not profess to be a prophet and I don't know if this will make sense to you but God keeps saying, "you've been silent too long"." Can you imagine my reaction to her statement? Here I am minding my own business and God interrupts the scene. That is just like Him! The then local Killeen president of Wealthy Sisters Network, Lila Holley, was sitting next to me and I am certain she could "feel" my heart leap at that very moment. The tears began to flow as if a fountain had been turned on in my eyes. I could not help the emotional outpouring because I knew exactly what she, through God, meant. At the end of the breakfast meeting I was asked to close us out in prayer. The power of God enveloped me in that prayer. For me there was no one but God in the room with me. Since that time, personal attacks have gotten much stronger.

Rewind to June 2008, stationed in Hawaii. Seven years of living in Hawaii had many ups and downs. Have you ever sat in church listening to the Word of God, knowing that He is imparting/implanting/downloading in your spirit but you are held captive, unable to be free in the spirit? That was me. Just before our PCS to Fort Hood, TX God got ahold of me in service and shook some strongholds off me. Running around the church free to shout, clap my hands, give Him the praise: He was delivering me! I knew Fort Hood would be different and that it had some great things in store. I was not given what would be different at the time but I would soon find out. I had been accepted into the AMEDD Enlisted Commissioning Program in 2007 to go back to school and become a Registered Nurse. I knew my family and I would be moving to Fort Hood in June 2008 so I could begin school in August but God was up to something else.

Fast-forward to June 2010, full-time nursing student (while still drawing Army pay and allowances) about to enter my last semester before graduation: Husband announces the call to start a church and pastor. "What? Are you serious? Are you sure?" was my honest thought in that moment. "How could he be so inconsiderate" I said to myself in my then carnal mind. The pressures of school were weighing heavily on me. There were many sleepless nights due to taking care of home, husband, then 3-year-old daughter and 9-year-old son in sports and getting to study only after they were all fast asleep. God has such a way to reassure us though. To let me know that the church idea was His plan and not my husband's, God came to me that very night and spoke the name of the church to me. I awakened first the next morning and was downstairs at the dining room table when my husband came around the corner and said the SAME NAME: Tower of Faith. He said that was the name he was given. At that moment I could do nothing but agree and say yes Lord. When you have gone so long under the burden, the curse of what others' opinions, how they may feel about your assignment, your calling, your purpose, it is at times hard to break free in your own mind. Witnessing this very thing in my childhood plagued me. Fear held me captive. It gripped me far too long. I did not recognize this generational curse until it was already upon me.

Trying to please others who do not entirely have God's heart or vision will not get you closer to God. It will in fact drive you FROM Him if you allow it. It became hard to even pray, read my Bible, meditate on His goodness, grace and mercy He had given me daily. I was taking the attacks personally; however, had I been in the Word and praying like I knew to do I would have realized that Ephesians 6:12 NIV was indeed true. "For our struggle is not against flesh and blood, but against the rulers, against the authorities, against the powers of this dark world and against the spiritual forces of evil in the heavenly realms."

You see the captor disguises himself in many ways. He sets up shop in your closest family and friends so that you feel distanced or isolated when time has come to be free in mind, body and spirit. Others may not believe what you have to say but I must say that being in God's Will, His purpose for your life is so very important and must supersede ANYTHING else you may want to pursue. Be led by God. Psalms 119:133 NLT says "Guide my steps by your word, so I will not be overcome by evil. "

Far too often we quote scripture to fit what we want but don't take the WHOLE Word.  Psalms 37:4 AMP says "Delight yourself in the LORD, And He will give you the desires *and* petitions of your heart."  This is wonderful; however, we often fail to take the whole loaf and eat all of it! What do I mean by that? I, like many of you, ran with that piece of the scripture but forgot about the rest, believing we could do things our way and see positive results in the end. We may see some good but it will fail eventually. Things will fall apart.

So here is the scripture to keep in our minds and hearts in Psalms 37: 3-8 AMP: **3 Trust [rely on and have confidence] in the LORD and do good; Dwell in the land and feed [securely] on His faithfulness.⁴ Delight yourself in the LORD, And He will give you the desires *and* petitions of your heart.⁵ Commit your way to the LORD; Trust in Him also and He will do it.⁶ He will make your righteousness [your pursuit of right standing with God] like the light, And your judgment like [the shining of] the noonday [sun]. 7 Be still before the LORD; wait patiently for Him *and* entrust yourself to Him; Do not fret (whine, agonize) because of him who prospers in his way, Because of the man who carries out wicked schemes.**

Placed in context, His desires will become ours when we follow His way. Then and only then will He honor the desires of our heart.

Transition time: Freedom as defined by the Merriam-Webster dictionary is the quality or state of being free: the absence of necessity, coercion, or constraint in choice or action. *It is also defined as* liberation from slavery or restraint or from the power of another. It is independence *or* the quality or state of being exempt or released usually from something onerous. Another definition states that it is the quality of being frank, open, or outspoken. These definitions are bold statements of character. The bible gives many words of wisdom to get and remain free.

The Lord's joy is your strength so when Satan comes to tear you down, tell him to get under your feet. You are more than a conqueror!

I am so grateful that His grace IS sufficient for me and you. I have found grace after forgiving the one who hurt me in many ways. I now fully rely on and trust in God.

John 16:33 NLT says "I have told you all this so that you may have peace in me. Here on earth you will have many trials and sorrows. But take heart, because I have overcome the world." What a comfort!

**John 14:1 KJV. "Let not your heart be troubled; ye believe in God, believe also in me. 27. Peace I leave with you, my peace I give unto you. Not as the world giveth, give I unto you. Let not your heart be troubled, neither let it be afraid."**

Here Jesus is talking to His beloved disciples. Notice that he used the exact same words at the near end of the chapter as He used in verse one. Anytime something is repeated or emphasized, it is something of value, something to be remembered because it will be TESTED!

The Lord is my light and my Salvation, whom shall I fear? All that you have, all that you are belongs to God anyway so just surrender your will to His. Get rid of the fear and replace it with faith. When you do, you will be surprised at how He moves!

If you have low self-esteem, know that you are fearfully and wonderfully made. There is no one on this earth that can replace you. The gifts and talents He gave you are YOURS and they were given to you NOT for you, but to help someone else along the way. You are to also give God the Glory for His working through you.

Notice I am sticking with God's Word. When all else fails, when the world is in an uproar as it is now, when the spouse is gone and we are left to face reality, when our children have long left the home and are "doing their thing", when we don't know what to do or where to turn, His Word NEVER FAILS.

He said He would never leave us or forsake us even until our last breath.

**Joel 2:25 The LORD says, "I will give you back what you lost to the swarming locusts, the hopping locusts, the stripping locusts, and the cutting locusts. It was I who sent this great destroying army against you."**

I look forward to what comes next for me, come along! It took me almost two full years to fully walk in my calling but I am here now. I won't turn back! My life is just beginning and I look forward to all He will do through my life.

Mark 5:41 NIV states He took her by the hand and said to her, "Talitha Koum!" (Which means "Little girl, I say to you, get up!") See? Talitha was dead in her home, waiting to be healed. Her parents simply believed that Jesus could make her live again even against all odds. Those around them did not believe.

You may have been wounded, persecuted for speaking up for righteousness sake, stabbed to the point of death but ARISE, move from fear to freedom. Get up from that place of fear, disappointment, discouragement, depression. You have a call on your life too. You may not know it but ask the Heavenly Father His Will for your life. If you do not have a personal relationship with Jesus that is my first appeal to you: for Salvation.

He said in Roman 10:9 -10 NIV that if you declare with your mouth, "Jesus is Lord," and believe in your heart that God raised him from the dead, you will be saved. For it is with your heart that you believe and are justified, and it is with your mouth that you profess your faith and are saved. After you have received Him, find a local church where you can learn His ways and precepts. I am available to you and I would love to hear your great news! Congratulations, you have arrived at FREEDOM. Do not go back.

Don't allow the circumstances, the worry, or the fear to define you. Move in what God has for you, what He says is possible and what is YOURS. You are truly free in deed. I am free in deed. God bless you!

Shirley La Tour is a native of Ft Wayne, IN and has lived in many states by way of military, now residing in Killeen, TX. She graduated from the University of Mary Hardin-Baylor with her Bachelors of Science in Nursing and is licensed and board certified as a Medical-Surgical Registered Nurse. Soon to retire after 20 great years of service in the United States Army as a Captain in the Army Nurse Corps, she is a Certified Life and Health Coach, Co-Author in a Best-Selling and Award-Winning Book, first ever released by a collaboration of African American Active Duty Service members, Veterans and Retirees called *Camouflaged Sisters*!

She has been featured on such radio shows as KRGN 98.5FM and 'In Session with the Camouflaged Sisters'. Also a Speaker, Home Based Business owner, Founder of Walk It to Health walk group, Founder of Coming Out of the Shadows Women's Outreach Ministry (just had first event August 13, 2016!), wife and mother of two, Shirley is a force to be reckoned with!

Her passion is helping others realize their dream of good health inside and out without conventional medicine. She is a firm believer that God can and will do the impossible in every area of life for those that truly believe His word. She believes that God placed everything we need for good health here on earth and uses natural supplements along with good nutrition and exercise to help bring the body back to optimum health.

She does health related assessments, prepares meal plans, health coaching, and has natural supplements to get you on your way back to health! Weight management programs available. She is always willing to reach out to others in need of physical, spiritual or financial health.

She is an entrepreneur at heart, an avid volunteer in the surrounding communities and seeks to expand her reach around the world! With God, ALL things are possible. "To God be the Glory!" To learn more, visit www.shirleylatour.com.

# Dormeka Pearce

**I AM HEALED**

I woke up at 3:44 am to my same heartache. When I opened my eyes I was reminded that I was yet and still living with emotional pain. This topic is not easy to write on because it is a subject very dear to my heart. It is a message of healing! A message of redemption and a one of God's love. There are times in life that we feel lost, confused, depressed, abused, misused, and lonely.

We more than likely have experienced a terrible hurt! You know that type of hurt that interrupts your sleep and causes great pain and results in your spirit being heavy, a heartache! Maybe it was a divorce, a bad breakup, a friendship loss, death, abuse, betrayal, or rejection. These hurts may be setbacks to you but do not lose hope because there is a King of hope. I want you to know that all types of hurts lost their power over you at the cross! You are loved and you are worthy of whatever God calls you to do! Your healing is available today by faith.

I honestly believe that God wants to heal every hurt. He wants to bind up every wound. That emotional pain, wounded-ness, and hurt was taken care of in God's redemptive plan because he knew and he knows that we will experience it and that we need the supernatural power of his Son's blood to overcome pain! The bible says that he binds up our wounds. He is available to heal you no matter what you have gone through. God is near to the broken hearted and saves the crushed in spirit. If you have a crushed spirit, God desires to SAVE you! Have you ever had a broken spirit that was crushed by failure, God desires for you to accept his salvation and he desires for you to be rescued from the emotional bondage of hurt. Now, I'm not saying that you won't feel pain when something is hurtful but what I am saying is that you should not continue on living with hurt. If you experienced something painful 30 years ago, 20 years ago, or even 5 days ago, you should make steps towards a process of healing.

Don't wallow around in it until you develop a spirit of hurt and you perceive everything as hurt and lack coping skills to deal with tough situations. This is what the enemy wants to do to you. He desires for you to walk around wounded and broken. Living with a hurt spirit can cause you to spiral down into depression, suicide, and all forms of mental illnesses because you can no longer function properly in society. Those that carry hurt in their spirits often never bounce back fully from emotional trauma unless they have help to do so. For example, when I was a child I had something very traumatic happen to me that caused me to develop a hurt spirit, (I truly believe that childhood is where most of our problems take root), I would often cry for nearly any reason, I would buckle under pressure, I perceived lost as rejection and I would deal with acceptance issues, I could not cope with rejection or mistreatment,

I later in life developed depression and tried to commit suicide. The hurt I felt in my heart far outweighed my desire to live. This is the story of many individuals in America today. Sometimes a story takes time to unfold, whether it is good or bad. I later had to become rooted in God's love for me and although I am not perfect, I recognize that I have grown tremendously. But I had to first began to tackle the tough issues in life. It doesn't have to take long. Trust him! You will be 3 steps in front of everyone if you decide to look at your heart. If that is you, (A person that is dealing with emotional trauma) I want you to dare to believe the Lord to heal you from current and past wounds. Don't put a Band-Aid over your wound by ignoring it and simply functioning around it. Deal with those tough issues in your life and overcome the enemy by speaking words of life to yourself and having hope that things will get better, because they will! I know that many times my husband and I had to deal with things that were issues that stem from our families. We often look at the people that are related to us and know that they have not allowed the Lord to heal wounds from childhood.

This contributes to family problems that if not addressed properly could cause issues for the rest of our lives. However, the bible says that our latter days shall be greater than our former! Believe that and walk in it! I don't care what you did in the past, I don't care who you used to be, or what your struggle is, repent and believe you are LOVED! According to Colossians 2:15 Jesus spoiled every demon and made a show of them openly! This means that whatever hurt you are dealing with it has ALREADY been defeated! All you have to do is walk in the authority Jesus gave you. Your heart could have been broken yesterday but your tomorrow is always bigger than your yesterday. Your freedom is around the corner! Keep moving and you will walk into it!

For those that are dealing with childhood hurts or reoccurring hurts. I want you to know that God loves you! Here are some tips to help you overcome a trauma and other forms of emotional wounds, (1) be transparent with God, yourself, and someone that you can trust. Although God already knows what happened, he likes to hear you voice it and come to him for healing. You can't heal from something that you consistently put a Band-Aid over. Doctors don't put Band-Aids over deep wounds. They clean those wounds out and the stitch the wound up with care. Allow the holy ghost to dig into why you are living with hurt and to stitch your wound up with love. Receive healing when you pray. Ask the Lord to heal you and believed it is done!

Your freedom is around the corner! If someone did you wrong, (2) forgive them quickly! Forgiveness is for you and the person that offended you. Releasing them of their debt allows God room to bless you. Don't live in offense. It opens you up to tormenting spirits like fear, worry, rejection, and distrust. If you forgive you are shutting the devil's plan down! Now, this does not mean that you have to trust the person again or that you don't have to confront them. Sometimes confrontation is necessary. This too is an issue, being passive aggressive towards people will only create greater secrets.

Learn to confront the situation. Learn to be bold about what is done to you because you are worth it and most importantly forgive yourself! If God is not holding anything against you then you should not hold anything against you! You are FORGIVEN! (3) Read God's word and know you are loved and worthy. The bible says that we are to be rooted and grounded in HIS LOVE! When you think about how much God loves you, you are sowing seeds into your spirit to become rooted. This enables you not to be easily moved by offense and hurt. If a tree has deep roots, then it cannot easily be uprooted. The deeper the roots the taller the tree. If your roots are deep into the ground, then you are on the way to success. (4) Think on good things. A lot of mental torment is present because of what we are thinking about. Think about good and pure things. Do not rehearse the hurt in your head and try to move on from it. You are a blessing! Think about all the good that the Lord has done in your life. Think about what makes you happy. Think about God's goodness. The word says think on things, whatever is pure, whatever is lovely. Think on those things! (5) Surround yourself with positive and uplifting people. If someone is abusive to you, mistreating you or belittling you, do not stick around. You deserve better! You deserve to be treated with love and respect!

If they are mistreating you and doing you wrong it is an indication that they have issues and that you need new companionship in friends or possibly even a spouse. Pray for them. But find yourself some people that love you for you. That you can be real with. This helps in the healing process. Your heart is precious to God and it should be precious to those that are around you.

Hurt does not have to keep you down! The lord wants you to wake up with JOY! He wants you to live out your destiny. You have a purpose and a plan greater than your now! Love, live, and walk in your destiny because you have one! Remember, your freedom is only one step away and your fears are only an illusion!

The Lord is near to those who have a broken heart, and saves such as have a contrite spirit. Psalm 34: 18

Dormeka Pearce is a Christian writer. She shares both insight from experience and biblical knowledge. She is the wife of Matthew and the mother of Zoe, Matt Jr., Landon, and Israel. She is a successful blogger at She Builds a House. She is a student of God's word, stay at home mother, and serves as the Sr. Editor for BY Publishing and Rhonda Branch Ministries.

# Karen Tants

**Metamorphosis** *my struggle from darkness to light*

When I was little I was painfully shy, detached and had great difficulty making friends, so I stood back from everyone in school, especially if they were unkind to myself or others. I was quite often moody and used to sometimes feel that a dark cloud had control in my mind like a 'stand-over man', but that deep down inside I had a hidden power and I was part of something great, free, and full of love, but I was unable to break through. I recall one occasion where I was asked a question and the thought *'no'* formed instantly in my mind, but the word *'yes'* somehow came out of my mouth as if the intuitive wisdom within me had no voice and no way to express.

Although I was perfectly fine and happy within the comfort zone of my family and close friends whom I knew well, school on the other hand was like a nightmare where my social anxiety kicked in and I played small, erecting a boundary of aloofness which made me seem ignorant and rude on occasions. I guarded my personal space with a passion. An uncle or my grandad, can't quite recall, used to quite often say to me *"penny for your thoughts"*, whenever he visited.

An interesting thing is whenever I responded to anyone in frustration or anger, or even in normal conversation, sometimes my responses could be taken as double entendre, and this I knew after I spoke them while I 'listened'. It was almost like I was channeling without my judging good or bad.

I had no filter and the responses could be taken either way. The real me felt like an observer, unseen and unheard It seemed like an unseen stronger power had a hold of me. I wanted so much to include myself with friends but I was not strong enough to overcome a deep fear of expression, expecting rejection. I was beset by fear and anxieties, subsequently affecting interactions with teachers and my peers, whilst creating for myself a mental hell.

I was often told *"don't worry, it may never happen"*. In my teenage years I rebelled, gave my parents a very difficult time at one stage and did some wrong things for which I was rightly punished. Feeling a deep knowing that I had a higher purpose and I was not living it, I often prayed to be a better person. I prayed for wisdom, and prayed to uncover the truth and meaning of my life. Even though I suffered internally, to this day and for as long as I can remember, instances of bliss and joy filled me from within. Lasting briefly each time, it gave me strength, instilling in me a deep faith, and freedom in the knowing that we are all a part of something great; inner knowing instances when I felt free, whole, and completely loved and embraced by God.

After two failed marriages; my first husband cheated on me numerous times, my second husband was verbally abusive and I went through a very difficult period leading to much self-searching. I slowly began to realize that my life experiences were perfectly guiding me to learn to love myself. As a result of this realization I embraced my shadow side, transforming it in the process. I learned to look *inside* of myself for love, rather than from *outside* of myself, (from others). I planted the seeds of self-love, and on wings of God's grace they grew. I was able to give expression to my Soul, subsequently shifting the poles of my perception. By tapping in to my subconscious potential, I illuminated and gave birth to walking in God's grace. *"Love is letting go of fear."* -Jerry Jamplosky.

My inner metamorphosis came with spiritual dream visions and initiation experiences beginning around 2005 when my youngest son started his schooling and I was guided to study psychic development, tarot and subsequently followed my healing path. I began to search and read lots of books by popular and not so popular spiritual authors, and would often have five or six books open at the same time. If I came to a block in my mind, I would leave that book and read something else until I was ready to release it.

This happened particularly whilst reading 'Entering the Castle' by Caroline Myss.

Going back to the metamorphosis vision experience, I found myself in a beautiful fluorescent bright and colorful energetic bubble. It was similar to a tunnel, the tunnel turned and I was moving along within it. I had the awareness that I was exiting this bubble through an opening that was very small and confining, the timing was precise for it to open and it did I made it through. Another awakening vision experience around that time, I had the urgency to put on my shoes; as I was putting them on, I heard a voice say *"It's time"*, then I felt and heard electricity enter through the top of my head. I feel that these two experiences were connected with a spiritual re-birthing process, or initiation. Since then I have documented countless transformational dream visions in a healing journey that is the subject of my fourth book to assist others to self-realization from my own personal experiences, and from the teachings I have received from spiritual masters.

Writing down my thoughts, inspirations, dreams and visions were an important step to finding my purpose and freeing myself from fear to embrace freedom. When you journal, it does not matter if no one reads your writing expressions, the important step is to write it all out onto paper and out of your head. You can burn it afterwards if you wish to; this in itself is healing as you can build a sacred fire, bring the phoenix in as the symbol of re-birth and transformation, then let it all go. Writing provides a release, so that God can fill the space left in our mind with His responses; it leaves us open to healing flow from our higher self-connection to our source which is one with God. It is always, and only, between our individual self and God. Every single other person is a messenger from the same God within us all. Every other soul, is a messenger sent by self and in which we are all contained, we never left. Knowing this is incredibly freeing.

The part of us that is seeking, is the part of us that is real, (soul calling) and calls us to realize that life on earth as we know it is a stage play that we each play a part in. To play our part, we sometimes have to provide each other with hard and difficult lessons. Most often we do not know this on the physical level, it also explains why we cannot fathom when sometimes we do the things we do, but every move we make in thought, word and deed, both positive and negative expressions, is directed by God. The more we vibrate in this awareness, the easier life appears and the more at peace we feel. Non-resonant frequencies fall away and our soul no longer needs those experiences to learn from. We create peace (order) in our life rather than war (chaos).

Following are five key points that I wrote out for this anthology based on my own fears as an example:

- **Self-reflection** to identify the root cause of a fear, knowing that the answers are within. My issues as an example: 1. Self-expression (what others may think) 2. Fear of alienation if actions are not socially acceptable, or what others may expect of me. 3. A need for acceptance of Me. 4. Afraid to be 'different'. 5. Afraid to share my heart, my love, my Divine expressions. 6. Afraid to push boundaries. 7. Afraid of own power, fear of success. 8. Self-sabotage.
- **Calling** on Higher Self and the forces of Divine help to help overcome fear.
- **Unearthing** my hidden desires to realize my passions and higher purpose.

> **Identifying** the dynamics of the comfort zone, which is nothing but a glorified rut that prevents one from growing, living, or serving others. It is given a name that seems inviting, so you enjoy living there, being there. It is an ego trap.
> **Facing** my fears head on, just doing it, just being there, just turning up, and allowing for God to work out the details for the best outcome.

Embracing the contrast is something that I have worked on for years now, owning my own shadow and no longer blaming outside circumstances for my inner struggles. I have learned that without the contrast we are unable to experience or fully appreciate the dynamics *leading up to*, or even understanding the difference *within* the dynamics which enables us to have positive relationships with others *going forward*.

I have learned that forgiveness, gratitude and taking responsibility for our own life and circumstances, acknowledging our negative aspects not just the positive, is how we go through our traumas to the blessings and gifts that lie within them. Without the darkness we cannot recognize Our Light, and if we desire to change, the way to reach it is by doing the deep inner work on ourselves at the source where we create on the subconscious level.

The ability to reason, a sense of gratitude, forgiveness, appreciation, openness and ownership of own responsibility opens the 'metaphoric' doors and windows of being to receive positive experiences and healing. This creates a space, or 'state' of Grace through which we begin to resonate and reach out to the space of Grace in others and unite with a Divine magnetism; when we share openly from our heart space, it creates an energetic space for others to open up to their own heart light. To feel safe in expressing and to receive a positive result is impossible if an understanding space is not provided or allowed. Opening your own heart provides that healing space for others to grow and blossom into their own empowerment and connection to God.

I would like to share my thoughts on empowerment and what it means to me, focusing on the key words for this anthology that has come to me to share. Fear and love cannot co-exist. When we are in fear, we have rejected love. Love vanquishes fear, therefore whatever you do and however life treats you, learn to take love with you and be love itself. Love enables empowerment, and empowerment is freedom wherever you find yourself.

Calling on Divine Presence helps to prevent being overwhelmed when a lot of openings and pathways appear at the same time. Presence helps you to re-center to come from a space of truth and love. Fear is the opposite of love, and love is the 'road' to freedom. Faith is inherent to achieving a feeling of freedom. Faith and freedom go hand-in-hand. Freedom is trusting (faith) in the universal process of life, and faith rests in the knowing of a Higher Power (God) who's life force flows and vibrates to create a balance that *moves* within all creation.

In conclusion, the following writing is an excerpt of some deep wisdom spoken by Jim Carrey. Some of you may have already heard this but it bears repeating especially for this wonderful anthology:

*"We are not the avatars we create, we are not the images on the film stock, we are the light that shines through, all else is just smoke and mirrors; distracting, but not truly compelling.*
*Why not take a chance on faith? Not religion, but faith. Not hope, but faith. I don't believe in hope, hope is a beggar; hope walks through the fire, but faith leaps over it. Our eyes are not only viewers; they are also projectors that are running a second story. The picture that we see in front of us all the time, fear is writing that script!*

**Now fear is going to be a player in your life, you get to decide how much. You can spend your whole life imagining ghosts, worrying about the pathway to the future, but all**

*there will ever be is what is happening here, and the decisions that we make in this moment, which are either based on Love, or fear".* **Jim Carrey**

I would like to take this opportunity to thank Sundi Sturgeon for inviting me to author here, and to Teresa Hawley Howard for the wonderful work you do and for the chance to share my story in this anthology with all you amazing authors. My sincere wish is that my personal account will inspire and guide the readers who may be struggling at this time, and whom may feel similar associations with my own struggle.
With God's Love, infinite blessings to you all.

I am a wisdom seeker. I have a deep desire to raise my consciousness to the level of soul expansion, and to serve and act for the highest good. I desire oneness with God while still in the physical to be able to act as a force for good in this world and beyond by being an embodiment of compassion and wisdom in action.

I have undertaken my healing path, and know that the path to healing is with Self; we can only be a bridge for others to remember that all healing comes from God within each of us, and that bridge is unique for each One of us.
I love to read spiritual books and have many master teachings among my collection although many I have either re-sold, given away or lent to friends and like-minded others. Currently I am studying the SRF Lessons through Self-Realization Fellowship, the teachings of Paramahansa Yogananda.

I express myself fluently more through my writing in my own private space rather than the spoken word in a room full of people. My discovery, or feeling behind this as I write this bio is it is difficult for me to speak in truth while faced with illusory bodies and masks that hide true Identity, knowing the true Identity is hidden in both Self, and all others, knowing it is all an act. I feel and now understand that you can *Be* in truth without saying a single word. The word is the energy you emanate and resonate with. Unspoken. I would like to add here that my current husband Jim's song for us, our song, is *When You Say Nothing at All* by Ronan Keating.

I am the self-published author of *Soul Magic - spiritual alchemy* published in 2012. *In Silence your Garden Grows* published in 2013 and *In the Presence of Angels* published in 2014. My books are available on kindle for all mobile devices, and in paperback, from Amazon.com in all countries where Amazon is available.

A wife, mother and grandmother, I live in Central Victoria, Australia. Thank you for reading, Karen G Tants
Reiki & Seichim Master Teacher-practitioner
Member of SRF (self-realization fellowship) My Facebook pages: **Heaven's Healing Angels, The Wisdom Portal, Freelance Book Writing and Editing Services**

# Vicki Cruz

**Whom the Son Sets Free**

As I share my testimony with each reader, I write in a sweet upmost sense of Freedom which came from different types of bondages that I have been delivered out of in my lifetime of 43 years. In my Fear to Freedom story, I will share the fear of letting go and being alone. The what and how I was broken from it all the negative emotions that spiraled from fear and the importance to taking heed of your own mind and emotions.

I give Glory to God who has blessed me with the ability to recognize His presence and the ability to make my way back to the Garden where He designed us all to be. I also give Jesus Christ the Glory because of His obedience and willingness to hang on the cross, naked and unashamed for me which has allowed me the ability to write and share my life with each of you unashamed with the hopes and desires that my personal experience would set you free and increase your desire to wholeheartedly commit and desire nothing but He who died for us and lives in us.

Just as our Redeemer came to fulfill His destiny to giving us eternal life, we each, like Him must carry our Cross and be crucified with Christ as stated in Galatians 2:20 (NIV) I have been crucified with Christ and I no longer live, but Christ who lives in me. The life I now live in the body, I live by faith in the Son of God, who loves me with an everlasting love and gave himself for me. I pray that as you read and understand how deception lured and trapped me into different types of fears and also placed bondage through my mind and by God's Word as the deceiver did to Jesus in the desert. BUT GOD, a Faithful Heavenly Father who kept me in perfect peace, giving me hunger to want to know and grow in HIM and HIS Word, and most importantly believing what the blood of Jesus which was poured for me so I can have free life here on earth and eternal life in Heaven.

### Fear of Letting of Go – A Marriage Vow

I had recently come to surrender my life almost two years prior to our separation/divorce and falling in love with God daily. Our ninth year marriage anniversary day was spent at a funeral home pre-planning our funeral arrangements and plots as it was my plan to forever be married to my husband. My husband turned to me and said, are you sure you want to be here and not dinner somewhere? Being that there was a pre-arrange funeral special being offered and trusting that my marriage would be a forever thing, I said let's not pass this offer up and begin to prepay expenses early.

Deep inside I felt my husband drifting away a bit and doing unusual things like not wanting me around family events. (We will leave the unusual details in the past where they belong.) During this time, I came to know Christ at a deeper level and took my marriage vows to a deep understanding along with my role as a submissive wife praying for my husband's salvation daily. This was also a time of my life where God's Grace became more relevant to me along with giving me the understanding that the ability to change only came through the Power of Blood of Jesus.

The traditional wedding vows pledged at the early age of 19 was embedded in my commitment when I said "I do" after dating for a year and a half. Granted our vows were made in front of a judge one day before his six month US Navy deployment. I took heed to the well-known scripture Matthew 19:5 (NIV) and said, 'For this reason a man will leave his father and mother and be united to his wife, and the two will become one flesh'? It was almost ten years of marriage, when I lost my best friend and husband, father of our three children, the man whom I thought I would share the rest of my life with, raise our babies and grandchildren together. One of the most difficult and extreme painful event in my life - until death is what I anticipated.

This commitment was a forever deal and absolutely no way I could or should let go after all God said, he hated divorce. Written in Malachi 2:16 (NIV) "The man who hates and divorces his wife," says the Lord, the God of Israel, "does violence to the one he should protect," says the Lord Almighty. So be on your guard, and do not be unfaithful.

Please note small disclosure, that my story, by all means is never to bash my former husband, the father of my children who is an excellent father and was a provider for our home, however deceived to the astray and lacked in the protection of our covenant and walk with God. We today, after 14 years of being divorced have remained cordial and amicable for our children sake. This story is to reveal my story, how deception persist and freedom prevails.

### What was a really afraid of?

Who would have known that mid-summer that year I would be clinging to my husband's knees begging he not leave me and our three babies, that I would do anything to save and keep him from not going to the arms of another woman. This painful dreaded day was one where I felt I was on the Cross at Calvary and crucified with Christ. The greatest challenge was *so hard to let go,* woman or no woman, I would accept and endure the infidelity.

Deceived thinking that holding on was the right thing to do in hopes that he would change his mind and not leave. I didn't understand that deep inside of the root I was afraid to let go, I was afraid *of the change* and to allow God to move in our behalf or better yet, my behalf. I held on to bible scriptures that gave me most comfort to avoid the what next and the pain to come. It was at the very moment in which God spoke to my Spirit and said, "LET HIM GO." I digested those words for several minutes as every part of body felt anguish of the unknown ahead. My faith in God the morning of was a child-like faith that the willingness to be obedient was simple. But not this time, not this dreadful moment. I begged God and tried every bit to compromise, but knew that His way was the only way.

## Trusting God's promise

I wiped off the tears, accepted my husband's decision and allowed him to walk out of our home we purchased together two years prior. I took a took a deep breath, inhaling God's unconditional love, and a second-deep breath, inhaling God's promise in scripture Jeremiah 29:11 (NIV) which reads, For I know the plans I have for you," declares the Lord, "plans to prosper you and not harm you, plans to give you hope and a future. My child-like faith trusted every promise God wrote in His Word and gave me a perfect peace into my heart knowing that my option was to stand alone in physical, however I was never alone because He would never forsake me Deuteronomy 31:6 (NIV).

## Understanding and embracing my value

God revealed to me at the time my worth and value as His daughter and allowed me to look at my husband through His eyes. Forgive them for they not know what they do in Luke 23:34 (NIV). This scripture resonated in my spirit allowing me to see that what He saw in my husband. With the automatic of receiving of Grace, this scripture I was able to release and forgive both he and myself. It also allowed me to see the great father he was for my children and to teach my children the importance of them keeping the commandments in honoring their daddy as written in Exodus 20-12 (NIV) which reads: Honor your father and mother, so that you may live long in the land the Lord your God is giving you. In which today, 14 years later my adult children, continue to honor and love their daddy to the fullest. They have been blessed with an amazing step-mom and a little brother and sister.

### Fear of Being Alone

My pillows took a little bit of the many mixed emotions I felt the first two months of getting adjusted to my children being gone for the weekend. In the beginning, I had no idea that yet another change would occur. A change that would have me carry a strong sense of grief in my heart and also caused me to look back which opened and added salt to the wounds. Another moment in which led me to an opportunity to seek and grow in Christ, heed/fight with the Word again and remind myself that I walk in faith and not sight. It was scripture Philippians 3:14 (NIV) I press on toward the goal to win the prize for which God has called me heavenward in Christ Jesus which pulled me through to not look back but trust God was working it all out for my good because I love Him and have been called according to His purpose, Romans 8:28 (NIV).

### Loneliness

I could accept my husband being gone, but not my babies. Being a military wife, raising my little ones which at the time were 11, 8, and 5 years of age, day and night alone was all I ever knew to do. I was both a mom and a dad to my children I had no idea of what I was facing much less knew the ingredients to master loneliness. In my fear of being alone, I masked a couple of nights going salsa dancing with the girls, but only to come home feeling convicted and rebuking condemnation with the Word again. Standing on John 3:17 (NIV) For God did not send His Son into the world to condemn the world, but to save the world through Him. It would be like the enemy to lure us back into trying to fill the void with worldliness only to turn it against us. Again, not saying that salsa dancing is a sin, only that knowing that in my Spirit, I didn't belong there and was surely not reaping healing shaking and breaking on the dance floor. It was a temporary void and a time to look for venues to occupy my mind and time as I rested in Jesus and seek the Kingdom. Matthew 11:28 (NIV) "Come to me, all you who are weary and burdened, and I will give you rest."

## Dying to self

During this separation I was in school seeking to obtain my Bachelor's degree, which was completed in 2006 and in the United States Navy Reserves. Much of my time was filled by studying and serving weekend's working for our Country. It all began to make sense to me that I did anything and everything I could get my hands on not only because of knowing that I can do anything through Christ who strengthens me, but to avoid the dreadful pain inside. To avoid loneliness and realizing I had to die to the fear of being alone by facing the fear and be just that, ALONE. It was the first time in my life that I would go out to restaurants, grocery shopping, events and more all alone. Alone with God and my pillow, where I wept fearlessly, I hugged and even talked to my pillow. Finding myself in a place where I had to discover things to do with my time alone such as being with God, spending more time in ministry feeding homeless, praying at hospitals, serving anywhere and everywhere, performed physical fitness time for myself, and seek out friends and family. However, keep a balance and my heart before God.

## Be Stubborn for Christ, HE is Stubborn for you

Holding on to fear, leaves different doors open to our mind and/or Spirit. A weed that will grow and take residence in our spirit of you don't wholeheartedly surrender all to Jesus and allow Him to reign in and through you. Understanding that change may come with a ripple effect and that we should always prepare ourselves and trust that just as we serve a consistent Father God, that the father of lies is just as consistent. 1 Peter 5:8 (NIV) Be alert and of sober mind. Your enemy the devil prowls around like a roaring lion looking for someone to devour.  We as inconsistent humans have to be alert and girded.

As stubborn as I am, I am stubborn for Jesus and not allowing the Blood to drip in vein.  It poured for us all.  Trusting Romans 8:28 (NIV) And we know that in all things God works for the good of those who love him, who have been called according to his purpose.  As I type every word, I type from with a heartfelt and true brokenness allowing His Living Water pour into those willing to receive.  I pray my dear reader that as you experience any change or grief in your life from disappointments, you will come to the understanding that it is only through our Faith in God, His Spirit, His Truth and His Son that we can and will Overcome.  I believe in you and so does HE.  Our Father loves you so much at is written in John 3:16 (NIV).

Connect with Vicki:
vickicruz3987@gmail.com
832-859-3987

# Sheree Wright

**FOOD IS NOT THE ENEMY**

My battle with food consumed big parts of my life, stealing my joy, holding me back from the will of God and causing many emotional, mental and anxiety issues. My journey to freedom has been overwhelming and empowering. It takes constant surrender to God. I have no idea where I'd be if I did not decide to walk in the light and uncover this secret part of my life which was literally killing me a slow and painful death.

I am growing stronger on this journey in every area of my life and I owe it all to the new mercies available every moment of every day. I pray that God will speak to your heart through this story and bless you abundantly in everything you do.

Food is NOT the enemy

So I don't know when it started.
I don't know why.
But somewhere in my teens I came to love food so much, that it became an obsession and then that love turned into hate. A faulty relationship with something that's purpose is to nourish and strengthen you...turned into in a fight resulting in sickness and weakness.

My mind, body and spirit has been through a journey of trials that I still don't fully understand. But I know enough to share my story. I know enough to realise I'm not the only who struggles with these issues. And I know enough to realise that keeping quiet does not help anyone, it hurts. I know that my story is one of victory and I need to share it to encourage others who are fighting this battle.

Food is not the enemy.
I can't even remember what I first caused me to throw up. After it happened a few times I was off to the doctor with mum. I was 15.
There was no physical reason, I wasn't physically ill, didn't have any viruses or anything obvious causing me to vomit. They put it down to being a 'mental thing'.
I had no idea what was going on! I wasn't thinking "oh how about I just throw up now that I've had a meal with my family"

Bulimia.

Here is a label that put me in a box in which I didn't belong.
I wasn't concerned about my image.
I'd just got myself my first serious grown up boyfriend. Life was good. No traumatic experiences from my childhood. No drama happening in my life at that point.
My parents owned the small town general store. I had people skills, work ethic, I studied and did pretty well at school.
But every now and then, a little while after a meal, I'd vomit. I didn't force it, it didn't sneak up on me with nausea or any warning signs, I'd just feel so full, I'd bend over the toilet bowl and empty the contents of my stomach.

Just like that.

It gradually became more regular.
Doctors warned me off certain foods. Then they told me my trap door (it has a proper term but that's what I call it) wasn't closing properly, so I went in to have a camera

inserted to see if there were any deeper medical issues with my digestive system.

Nothing.
No explanation. No cause. No reason.
It must be in my head.
Counselling ... Ring this number.
My weight, energy and health slowly deteriorated.
Still no answers.
My family was good; my life was increasingly good. I was really confused.

I started obsessing over foods. Keeping a food diary. Good foods, Bad foods, right foods, wrong foods.

I started obsessing over my weight, the size of my waist, thighs, tummy. How much was on the scales, before a meal, during a binge and following a purge. I only know the meaning of the word purge because I read it in someone else's story of bulimia.

I started studying the condition - I still didn't understand, I didn't think I fit in that category, I didn't think I needed that sort of help, but I kept exploring anyway. It must be in my head.

It became less of an incidence of throwing up a meal and more of a tactical response system "I can gormandize whatever my taste buds desire, until I'm full to the brink, then I can empty out and start with a clean slate. I've got this under control. I'm ok."

This was now, not just a part of me, but it consumed me, literally. it took up my whole mind, physical being and soul. I was being crushed and victimized by my own self.

I was increasingly confused and guilt stricken that I couldn't "get it together" or just "snap out of it". I had an addiction to food that I couldn't overcome. Food is everywhere, I couldn't exactly abstain from it or go into rehab.

Every now and then I'd break free. Going days, leading into weeks without a binge episode. Then I'd come crashing down into a bulimic heap again and spiral into the darkness of my habit. Overwhelmed by emotions that I didn't understand. This cycle has been going now for 16 years. I am 31 years old. I'm not a teenager anymore, I'm not one of those girls in the stories... yet I find myself trapped in a war with food.

For the love of food ...
I mean hate.
I mean love.
Hate myself love food
Love myself hate food

I have juggled this battle for a long time (and I know I'm not the only one). Although it's a journey that's taught me so much, I still cannot quite explain it properly.

Bulimia.
There's that label again.

For me, not an issue with body image or self-love in a "worried about the way I look" sense.
More an issue with trying to be perfect but having low self-esteem, unworthiness, disrespect for myself and unable to control my emotions. Inside me, I'm tortured by my perfectionism thoughts. My need to control. My inability to look at the bright side of life.
I'd say it's 'negativity' mixed with a whole lot of 'MESSED UP'

It's believing the lies that are overtaking my soul and refusing to accept the truth.

It's not believing that I have purpose and value and gifts to offer this world.

Inside me is all this light wanting to shine brightly but I'm overshadowed by darkness.

Bulimia.

I can't even go into details about what it's like. It's too graphic. Too disturbing. And quite honestly - too shameful. Those who have suffered, you know what I mean.
Those who haven't, you don't understand and still won't understand even if I do explain in detail. So it's better left unsaid at this point. I will be as real as I can without grossing you out (that would be a whole extra book).

Bulimia.
I know I'm not alone.

Bulimia is:
This strange compulsion to eat loads of really poor quality food as fast as you can, spaced perfectly with water to keep a fluid consistency that is easier to bring up.

Bulimia isn't:
Enjoyable.
You can't really enjoy the feeling of eating while you're plagued with this uncontrollable guilt, shame and disgust at yourself for your actions that you seemingly cannot control at the time.


Here's my victory.
I've spent most of my life believing I don't have any enemies. When kids at school were bickering, I was the peacemaker. When family members weren't talking, I never held a grudge. I just can't bear the thought of being at war with someone and having enemies. Some people I knew had several enemies and went through life creating more. Not me. I did everything I could to avoid it.

If people didn't like me - I never hated them in return. I'd go out of my way not to give them any reason to hate on me. And I'd love them back.
I hate the word hate.

Then, as I spiraled into an eating disorder, Bulimia, I discovered a real enemy. I loved food so much, I developed patterns that led me to hate it & resent it because of what it was doing to my mind, emotions & body over time of abusing it.
I couldn't get away from food - so suddenly I was at war. Constantly.

A battle within my mind. Every moment of the day. Sometimes I'd find peace, but it was short lived & so war broke out again.
Food was my enemy.

My bulimia started at 15. I still don't know the original cause or reason for my behavior (Or condition, or illness, or whatever you want to call it) I don't like that I received a label for it & I came to realize later on, that the labelling & reading into it probably caused more problems to evolve and opened more doors to the lies.
I believed a lot of lies.
One of those lies being, food is my enemy.

FOOD is NOT the enemy.

I married my sweetheart at 20, always vowing to myself that I'd stop bulimia right away. Giving myself second chance number 872.
I was sick & tired of feeling sick & tired. I'd been on an emotional rollercoaster for 5 years and after several attempts at 'self-help' 'snap out of it' 'grow up' kind of approaches, I was beginning to think I'd never claim victory. My will to fight was deteriorating with every failed attempt to get over it.

I had support, I had so much love. There were no real reasons for me to be behaving the way I was & so while I thought there was something wrong with me, there was actually nothing wrong. I grew more and more resentful towards food & the fact that it ruled my whole life. I could not control this successfully on my own. I was still striving unsuccessfully at perfectionism.

When I was 25 we had our first child. I gained a whole new lease on life & suddenly found new respect for myself & repaired my relationship with food. For a while, it lasted good. Then for whatever reason- the enemy rose again. Trying desperately to destroy me & gaining ground fast.

At 27 after moving 1000km from our home & having our second child, I would say I was at my absolute lowest. Lost inside, feeling alone / separate & unable to call for help because I'd cried out so many times before. I was sure people were sick of picking me up out of my mess (coz I know I was exhausted of it). I especially pay credit to my husband who through each struggle was my rock and strength. Deep down inside, I was sure he'd eventually give up on me too.

I believed it was my battle to face.

Until something happened. Through connecting with a group of Christian women in our new town. I saw something I'd never seen before. A love and presence that I can't explain. I experienced what a commitment to Jesus Christ could do in my life & I surrendered.
I became a Christian. I didn't tell anyone, other than the Christians I was fellowshipping with.
My tendency to secrecy was with me & I was so afraid at what everyone else would think - or whether my new way of life would actually change me.

I had tried everything else before.
This. Was. Different.
This. Is. Freedom!

There is way more to my transformation than what I can share here, for the purpose of this WOMEN ON A MISSION project, I need to keep it brief and to the point.

As I began to walk in freedom & continue my journey to grow closer in relationship to God & understand my true identity in Christ I could see & feel incredible changes in every area of my life.

So, I became a Christian when we had our 2nd baby, I was 27 years old. Previously, I knew nothing of the Lord, nothing much about God except the thought "maybe he exists?!" I had never read the bible. I don't think I even payed attention at school in religion classes.
Nothing ever clicked. I had no reason to question my existence.
But by this point in my life, I was searching. My soul had copped such a beating that I knew, I just knew, there is more to me than flesh and blood. There's more to life than obsessing over food (for the sake of obsessing). I used food as my comfort, my emotional ricktor scale. If I was happy I'd celebrate and eat. If I was sad or lonely or emotional or just wanted to escape reality, I'd eat.
Eat.
Eat.
Eat!
All I ever seemed to do was eat!
And when I wasn't eating or throwing up, I was imaging what else I could eat. Sweet - savory - warm - cold - quick - complicated ...
O. B. S. E. S. S. E. D!! With food.

Food consumed me so much, I began to hate it.
It was stealing my joy, taking me away from the important things in my life, like being content and enjoying our kids and our marriage. Appreciation and gratitude for all the good things was marred by my distraction with food. This war inside me that nobody knew about or could ever understand.

I'd get so angry. So hurt. So confused. Lost. Alone. Isolated. Concerned. But unable to speak the truth.
I became an expert at hiding it. Hiding the evidence, hiding my feelings, hiding the fact that I needed help and was in deep deep trouble. I had an addiction. I had anxiety, depression and emotional stress. I felt like a real failure- so I wasn't going to tell anyone.

And besides, I've spoken out before. I got my little 'victory welcome home party' - you're free from that now - yay - what an achievement. Life goes on.
But I wasn't free. I never dealt with the root of the problem. I was more trapped than ever before and I didn't know how to get out.
I believed, I was too far gone.
I believed, I was a failure.
I believed I wasn't good enough, for love, for anyone's forgiveness or for anyone's understanding.
I believed food was to blame and food was the enemy. And I believed it was all my fault.

I believed the lies.
Food is not the enemy.

Through submission to the word of God and getting deep into relationship with Christ my Savior ...
My belief system changed.
My behavior changed.
My spirit being changed.
And through many trials & revelations I continue to change as I walk this journey in step with the most powerful guide & teacher.

My eating disorder controlled me against my will. A tactic of the enemy to use my weakness to destroy my soul and separate me from real life.
Christ loves me unconditionally & God has plans for me beyond my expectations. (This story, I believe being one of them).

JOHN 10:10 The thief comes only to steal and kill and destroy; I have come that they may have life, and have it to the full
JEREMIAH 29:11 For I know the plans I have for you," declares the Lord, "plans to prosper you and not to harm you, plans to give you hope and a future.

I've learnt I do have an enemy. The enemy to my soul is Satan- the devil. His plan is to steal kill & destroy & for me, he used food to manipulate me like a puppet & rule my mind & soul.

As I walk with Christ and stand on the TRUTHS in the word of God, I am free and have victory and no longer live in that darkness, but shine a light.

I no longer have to listen to, or believe, the lies.
Food is NOT the enemy.
With every thought that enters my mind I can compare it with the words of scripture and if it doesn't line up with the truth then I cast it out & it has absolutely NO POWER over me.

I am no longer afraid
I am no longer controlled.
I have victory and peace and an abundance of love that I cannot contain within myself.

This kind of love & selflessness needs to be poured out into the world, one broken heart at a time

I want people to know that they don't have to fight anymore.
This battle is not theirs to war in.
The victory is done & we've been set free. If we just surrender.

If you are suffering an eating disorder or any kind of anxiety, self-worth issue, bondage, destruction, addiction - whatever ... There is freedom for you too.

For every darkness there is light.
For every lie - there is a truth.
You choose what you believe. And FAITH cannot be taken away from you.

I urge you, choose life. choose to believe the TRUTH.
Because the truth will set you free.


You don't have to believe me. I'm not here to convince you of anything.
Ask God, Seek Him. He will deal with you. And he will reveal to you all things in perfect time. Open your heart and listen. It's a soft gentle calling that you won't want to miss!!

Romans 3:23 - For all have sinned, and come short of the glory of God;
John 3:17 - For God sent not his Son into the world to condemn the world; but that the world through him might be saved.

I am redeemed.
ISAIAH 43:1 But now, this is what the LORD says-- he who created you, Jacob, he who formed you, Israel: "Do not fear, for I have redeemed you; I have summoned you by name; you are mine
I'm not bulimic. I have experienced bulimia and I am redeemed.
My new identity is in Christ. And I stand firm on the truth of HIS WORD and PROMISE.

To the bulimic,
Don't waste your life on this.
It's too consuming
You're a smart girl
Don't be taking part in debilitating battles of the mind over Food!
FOCUS ON CHRIST

The word of God is so powerful.
HEBREWS 4:12 For the word of God is alive and active. Sharper than any double-edged sword, it penetrates even to dividing soul and spirit, joints and marrow; it judges the thoughts and attitudes of the heart.
Fill your mind SO FULL with His word that there is no room left for the ENEMYS LIES.
The enemy may have controlled you for so long, it's time to surrender over to Jesus and let Him take you over.

There's nothing more powerful than a submissive attitude to the one MIGHTY GOD who created us.

Remember, food is NOT the enemy.

_PRAY TO GOD
Acts 8:22 - Repent therefore of this your wickedness, and pray God, if perhaps the thought of your heart may be forgiven you.

Every day, hand it over to God. KNOW that you have no addictions, no cravings, you are free. It is not your struggle. PRAY OUT LOUD.

Lord, I know that this is NOT your plan for me. I know it's not the right thing to be doing, or the right attitude to have or the right way to treat myself and live my life. I don't want to struggle anymore. I need you Lord. I don't know how or why or where you are – but I choose to believe. I choose to trust. I choose life.

Please enter my heart right now, fill me up with your love and peace and overflow my mind and heart with revelation of who YOU are and how great you are and what amazing plans you have for my life. I NEED YOU. I surrender. Please forgive me for my sins, past present and future. Thank you for dying for me, forgiving my sins and giving me the gift of eternal life. I turn away from sin today and submit to you as

My Lord and Saviour. Thank you for leading me and guiding me in your way. The way of the truth. The way of life. AMEN.

It is not my strength that has caused me to gain victory in this battle. I want to make it very clear that it is the power of the Holy Spirit living in me who has changed the course of my life. and continues to change my walk. It was my choice to commit and put my trust in Jesus

Revelation 21:4 - And God shall wipe away every tear from their eyes; there shall be no more death, neither sorrow, nor crying. There shall be no more pain: for the former things have passed away.

Philippians 4:13 - I can do all things through Christ who strengthens me.

# Lisannia E. McIntyre

## "In the Midst of Chaos: I Found My Calling"

"What is Leadership? According to another fellow writer who prefers to remain anonymous from my professional leadership network, he describes "Leadership as an intangible asset that usually cannot be showcased through medals or plaques, as athleticism or aesthetic talent can". He further stated that "It is essential for the operations of any organization and corporation as well as for the successful completion of any project. He goes on to say that "If you know you've risen to the occasion to lead a group to success, you must demonstrate that you are qualified for other leadership positions". I finally got it; I had another Ah ha moment!

 This was the defining moment in my life and career that propelled me to do some soul searching about my stance in the leadership skills that laid dormant within me, due to the fear of the unknown. I quickly asked myself how will I make a difference? How can I implement my new skill set gained through real life experiences? Which in turn have changed and transformed my life in every level? The answer came to me almost immediately. Hence, I started to team up with other seasoned entrepreneurs to hone in the leadership strategies I needed to cultivate to better lead my tribe. As an emerging leader it is very important to understand what kind of leader we are; to better serve those we were called to serve. It's important to spend time daily educating ourselves through self-development. In Make Today Count; John C. Maxwell explains that it's necessary to sort out our values. I made it my commitment to lead others with the values I've embraced. The core values that I will like to focus on this chapter are as follows: family, freedom, time and my faith in God.

Family is the vessel that keeps everything in our lives fluid. When I speak about family. I am not only limiting to speak about relatives by blood but also family as in individuals whose kindness, love, and loyalty I received unconditionally during my current journey. I remembered being embraced with so much love and compassion in my darkest hours by total strangers who not only wished me well but helped me tremendously along the way.

This brings me to another point, in our rise to the top let us never forget to thank those dedicated individuals placed strategically in our lives to aid you to become a better you! I am also writing about freedom because many of us forget to continue to enjoy the simple pleasures of life as we climb the ladder of success. Hence, why the daily day to day can become cumbersome. In my experience, I implemented allotting time to enjoy nature, my children, worship, friends and being careful to add productive activities that stimulate the brain to function in its full capacity through renewed creativity. Lastly, but certainly not least my faith in God because he has given me the strength to persevere along with the like iron-will that won't succumb to the mediocrity of thinking, neither should you, my dear reader!

Do you ever wonder about what it takes to succeed? I never did, until faced with the most crucial moment in my life. It all happened so fast, I had lost track of time and dare to say even reality. My marriage to the "perfect man" was on the rocks; I woke up Christmas morning in a homeless shelter for women and children with my then Five-year-old Daughter and seven months old Son. Still in disbelief; somehow I was waiting for my guardian Angel to wake me up from this nightmare. Was I dreaming about when I was the Co- Star of the play "Bad Dream Reality" in college? Not a chance! I was awake, and this was very real. I then discovered, the right side of my face was paralyzed.

I remember, jumping up and down Rocky Balboa style. I was convinced, I was still asleep. I tried to smile only to realize that my smile was twisted and physically painful. I recall thinking, am I having a stroke or even worse a heart attack? I quickly got dressed and hurried to the hospital. I was registered and taken to the ER shortly after. Then the real adventure began, a series of test were performed to find a diagnosis. All major test was negative, my heart was strong and healthy. The ER nurse joked and said to me that my vitals were better than hers. Yet there I was sick and accepting my new reality. Life was crushing me to my core or so I thought! I remember, the doctor moving his lips telling me my diagnosis.

It was like the Charlie Brown effect when he said you have "Bell's 'Palsy". I was lost, he explained that it's a condition caused by inflamed nerves; causing my facial paralysis. I was prescribed steroids to help my condition and was told that for 80% of the cases it goes away but there is a dreaded 20 % chance that it may never go away. I literally felt like the Christmas Tree printed on my pajama top in that hospital bed. Before leaving the Hospital, I told the doctors that I was going to kick Bell's Palsy in the face. Smiled my twisted painful robotic smile and walked out determined to forge myself into the unknown and give it all I got, because what if? Never went to the arena to fight for what's right. I held my babies' little hands and promised never to give up!

Arrived at the shelter minutes later and resumed to opening our Christmas gifts. I refused to think negatively and continue to feel the fear threatening to take complete hold of my senses. It was finally official in my mind, I was going through a painful divorce and was homeless. I gathered myself and bravely promised not to look back, not even to take impulse. My head was feeling as dizzy as it did when my now ex-husband boxed me to the ground with three painful blows directly to my head. Somehow, I got up from that floor and fought back at the expense of nearly getting my neck broken back then.

But alas, that too is now part of my testimony. God's grace and divine protection wins every time. My face looked disfigured, I walked as if suspended by air due poor cognitive coordination due my condition. Inside my mouth felt disabled. I couldn't drink or chew without holding my jaw with my hands as I had no sensitivity on the right side of my face at all. By far one of the scariest and most difficult experiences to date in my journey to transforming my health, business, and life to success. I lost my clients, due my speech impediment. Yet, I was truly happy from within. I kept smiling my twisted upgraded smile, as I fondly joked about it, adding leverage for the sake of friends that were sad to see me with such disability. Needless to say, life became even more complicated.

Giving up? Not a chance! I knew that was not an option. I realized this journey was not about me, I had to remain strong for the sake of those whom I have been called to serve! As I shared precious moments with other homeless families, it all started to finally make sense. My soul was awakened, I understood the why in my trials, tribulations, and suffering. Rooted in this new found notion, my heart began to smile in a way that my physical body could not. Instead of hoping for a miracle to come I embraced my calling and started being that hope, light in the darkness and ultimately change needed in my homeless shelter and beyond.

 I was relentless, I made up my mind that absolutely nothing was going to stop me. I immediately took inspired actions, and founded my business while homeless; my inspiration came from sharing life with other homeless families. I got business cards and handed them out, determined to soon be able to offer them jobs. I became intentional about my goals and broke them down to weekly milestones achieving my business goals along with personal goals of self-sufficiency. I also became a proud graduate of the program offered to me and my family at the Sue Prudmore Shelter for women and Children; graduating with honors holding my life's baton in my hands again, and got back in the race; I signed my lease to my new happy place and continued to build.

I could hear the words of Zig Ziegler loud and clear in my subconscious when he said, fear has two meanings. "Forget everything and run" or "face everything and rise" The choice is yours! I choose to rise to the occasion. I now remember fondly, walking to take my kids to school, daycare and riding my blue bicycle to work. I even fainted shortly after selling my blood plasma to buy Diapers and wipes for my son. Through these trials and tribulations, I even self-represented myself and became stronger and was able to face my now ex-husband in court. I was awarded custody of my children along with one-year restraining order through a domestic violence injunction. Justice was beginning to be served, as I continued to heal.

Three months after the trial I was healed from Bell's Palsy. The struggle intensified, truly nothing worth having comes easy. I sifted through to the appearances of life to what truly is. Still, I hit rock bottom yet again and felt like the biggest loser because I had fallen prey to a scandalous scam. The authorities would do nothing about these scoundrels because I was gullible enough to make that bad investment. I then started working at a fast food restaurant and had a lot of fun doing it. While working at Checker's, I learned to flip burgers. There is no shame in earning a living with integrity while keeping my eyes on my divine mission. Currently, I am a proud business expert who delights in mentoring and training other entrepreneurs from different walks of life to fulfill their God-given purpose. What will you choose? I had so many doors closed in my face, yet I smiled. Shed many tears even, I simply had no time for self-pity. I found a new routine and committed to the new experience and self-discipline, no excuses. I started a whole new level of nutrition. Our body is designed to feel great! I learned to love myself enough to start and continue to live a healthy lifestyle. I also discovered, that by acquiring new hobbies: gardening and exercise. I was able to channel my worries and turned them into untapped creativity for my business.

By Spring of 2015, before the publishing of this book, for the first time in my life, I had flowers blooming in my first garden. I got beautiful Asiatic Lillie's. I became a happier person and forgot my condition altogether. I locked arms with people who wanted to do the same in their lives while having fun doing it; helping heal the world with their services and expertise. Before I knew it, my smile started peaking back. I had so much energy, it was hard retiring my brain to rest. I was pumped, my body was feeling and looking healthier than I've been this past 5 years of my life. It entered a new and exciting path that was allowing me to say goodbye to the old me and hello to the newly transformed me inside and out. I remember, my best Friend saying "whatever you are doing"? keep doing it, because it looks good on you! Yes, I was happy and on the road to recovery as well as enjoying true freedom to build back up with integrity. At last, my fears were conquered

I took back the reigns of my life and pursued a healthier lifestyle. Even though faced with the kind of adversity that cripples the mind, body and threatens the soul, I was not to despair. I now know what it feels to have lost it all while battling a disability alone in a homeless shelter with my two children; long court custody battles yet feeling like I had it all at the same time because I found myself in the midst of chaos, a leader was born!

Bell's Palsy made me weak physically making it almost impossible to focus due nerves dysfunction. But alas, I learned to become one with my disability and laughed at myself deeply during my journey of self-discovery in my life coach certification with the Southwest Institute of Healing Arts. Currently, I am healed and building back up with integrity in spite the odds in my Community of Hope.

Through perseverance and my faith in God, I am beating the curve of negativity and welcoming a new facet of my life that promises success beyond my wildest dreams as I live a life of purpose. Our mission is to empower 1 million women and families to self-sufficiency through education. Fast forward to today, I own a thriving home-based call center business. We service a wide variety of corporate clients. I also went back to school and currently pursuing a Master's Degree in Psychology with a concentration in Educational Leadership to better serve and understand my clients. I have teamed up with my community and have become an avid advocate for worthy causes in Education, Child Care services, and Domestic Violence.

 We are also in the product development phase of a breakthrough product that should be introduced to the marketplace soon. We have rallied against educational scholarship lawsuits for students and even sponsored pro-bono speaking engagements with the Early Learning Coalition in my adopted hometown.  What's next? In the near future, we look forward to opening a vocational Career Training Facility in Melbourne, Florida. We will offer a 90-day program free of charge to all individuals willing to commit, learn and make a difference in their lives.  We will provide, job offers after successful certification upon program completion.

Our services will be extended to other professionals worldwide through our online virtual learning services as well. Indeed, I can safely say that there are truly no failures in life only lessons to be learned. As an agent of change, leading by example while adopting a positive attitude clad with an iron will that is unshakeable and unbreakable has opened some innovative doors while embarking in new career interests as an activist, writer, and motivational speaker. I encourage you, my dear reader, to love yourself fiercely and more importantly to love every season of your life; embracing every experience as a lesson to be learned. In closing, I learned that "Interpersonal growth is manifested externally in its purest form when we learn to love and value ourselves against all odds."

Lisannia McIntyre's professional title is Owner- managing Director of PCS Management Group Inc. Her Professional client services home based call center, services various corporate clients via telephone and email support. She is also a member of the National Association of professional women; and was recently awarded the 2015-2016 Woman of the year circle award for excellence, leadership and commitment to her profession while encouraging the achievement of professional women. Lisannia is also an active member of the International Women's Leadership Association. She is currently pursuing a Master's degree in Psychology with a concentration in Educational leadership and intends to use it to better serve her clients and humanity.

She also attended Lynn University in Boca Raton Florida and obtained a bachelor's degree in International Business & a minor in marketing. Her mission is to empower 1 million women and families to self-sufficiency while achieving their personal goals and financial freedom. Lisannia plans to open a vocational career training facility in the near future to train, educate and give a hand up to less fortunate families in her community and hopes to take her vision internationally someday. She is also a mother of two amazing children Kya and Khaliq. In her spare time, she enjoys reading, writing, cooking, gardening, traveling and spreading the good news of the gospel of Jesus Christ to name a few.

contact@lisanniamcintyre.com
www.lisanniamcintyre.com

# Teri S. King

**BLUES TO GOLD**

It's hot in Texas, really hot! It's more humid than I've ever experienced, but I'm SO happy – well, now I am. It hasn't always been like this. I believe we all have our own journeys with trials and challenges that mold us into the people we are, here is a snippet of mine.

A little background might help. I grew up the only girl in a family of five boys who could do "no wrong". The boys, not me. Yep, I was the trouble child! My dad was an alcoholic who used his fists when he was unhappy - which was a lot! (he was a career mill worker with no understanding of how to get out). My Mom was a school teacher and a faithful Christian. Life has always been a tug of war between doing what I wanted and rebelling against the mainstream, trying hard to fit into a mold I neither understood, nor had the patience for. I was forever chasing the boys trying to join in on their adventures.

But I was "a girl" (whatever that was supposed to mean to my young ears) and would never be good enough to reach their level and do what they could do. I tried though! I would climb trees, raft down the river to the waterfall; I took up smoking (for one day until we got caught). My Dad always said, "She's more boy than all my boys put together". That's how he would introduce me in the bars to his friends. Like he was proud of me, my fight, and my ability to take a hit and get back up - to persevere. I used to find pride in that, until one day I wasn't sure it was a compliment. It wore me out, this battle of wills I fought, and really it was only with myself. Seriously, I don't think anyone else even noticed me.

I was often depressed and very sad and alone; so I filled my days with crazy pranks and adrenaline stunts – once again rebelling against the anguish in my soul and the expectations of those I loved. At 10 years old I took up gliding, joined a men's soccer league, hiked the Appalachian alone for days, ran away more than a few times – all just trying to get noticed. I was not this person they wanted me to be, polite, quiet, reserved and waiting. It was as if they were asking me to always wait. "When you get older", "When we do that as a family", "When you don't live under my roof". "What the hell was I waiting for?" was always my question. Why? For how long? For years I would stay to the outside of the crowd and only join in when cajoled to, but never really feeling as if I belonged.

Because I never belonged. Not really, not anywhere. Not in my family, not with the neighborhood kids, not at school and being alone I just questioned my existence more. Is there a purpose to my life? At 13 it was time to become a church member. So, I was asked to sit and speak with the church clergy to discuss God and my beliefs. I asked so many questions about faith and God and the Bible that my parents were called in and I was never confirmed in that church. Secretly, I think I made them start to question their own faith. (But that's probably just childhood reminiscing's) I questioned EVERYTHING. No one had answers, not ones that resolved anything for me, just created more questions.

You can probably imagine that I made life interesting by chasing so many crazy questions. And I did! I made sporadic, crazy decisions that would change my course 180° many, many times. I decided on a college on a Friday and moved 6 states away by Monday. I even got a scholarship from the church that disowned me! I took off to Hawaii two days after my brother got married. Yea, decided that one AT the wedding! I got married to a guy I met on a blind date – that didn't turn out too well. I was divorced soon after our son was born and we haven't really spoken since.

For five years after he first uttered the words "divorce", I would experience major life disasters every six months. I looked at this time as the beginning of the end.

I moved, and moved again, travelled a lot, and moved farther away from those I used to know. Part of me thinking I could just outrun myself and my fears. Yes, I was afraid. Afraid I was lost. Afraid I had no clue what I was doing, who I was, where I was going. I was afraid to even think about it, never mind put my fear into words or ask for help.

As the years passed, I matured but still had this sense of fear and loss. This empty hole inside that I couldn't seem to fill. I made it my "style", if you will, to make others happy, to wait on others, cater to make THEM feel worthy, and wanted, and happy. Maybe they had the answers? If I could just figure them out. If I just got close enough to someone who KNEW! I became the fun loving jokester you wanted at your parties. "No judgements here, just Love!"

But I was dying inside. I was dying a little bit more each and every day. I am Worthless! I have No Purpose! These were the words that would repeat themselves in whispers, and then in loud resounding shouts, throughout my head... all the time - all day long! Like drops melting off a roof on a cold winters day, forming a large, cold, hard, ice crystal. Building and growing with each depressing thought in my heart. "I could die and I wouldn't have made a difference." "What's the sense of my living?"

Until one day, not too long ago, I made a decision that would change my path forever. Time to just let go! Yes, to succumb to the negative voices coming from my heart! Yes, to erase the pain of feeling like I failed the game of life – I was a loser!

"Just admit it", my heart said. And that huge, hard, frozen piece of me, just dropped!

I took pills – lots of them – and waited for the blackness to just end it all. I was home with my boyfriend and we had fought over something I can't even remember now. It wasn't the fight; it was the feeling of loss again. I was insignificant. My thoughts didn't matter. I didn't matter. Not that I wanted to be dead, I just didn't feel I was supposed to be here. No sadness anymore, just acceptance of a sure thing.

But by God's mercy and maybe, as I wanted to believe in my heart, because I HAD made a difference in the world, I was found and taken to the Emergency Room. I was cared for there through the night and then sent to a Rehab facility to "deal with my issues". But I don't know if it was God's grace, or I was gifted a guardian angel or life is just more complex than we will ever really know – I KNEW. I just became aware of myself in a way I never had before. I woke up and had lost whatever crap I had been storing in my heart and my soul felt free. Maybe because I WAS wanted. Maybe because I felt a love I'd never felt before – guaranteed and unconditional. Maybe I was needed in the world, to have purpose and an impact. Maybe, just maybe, this game of life was NEVER over? I began to think the questions I had been asking WERE the answers and that I was doing it all right!

...And I was saved!

I felt as if this next "chapter", would be my defining and enlightened one. I started a new journey that I realized is about ME (and yours is about you!). Instead of rebelling against everything and giving of everything I had to others, I began researching and really paying attention to me, my feelings, how I react, or not, to everything. I asked NEW questions. Questions only about me and only to myself. I began listening to and reading motivational material and figuring out what made sense to me, what resonated within me. I kept positive affirmations around me. I began focusing on when I was negative (about anything), and changing it out with a positive.

I figured it's not about "fitting in" but more about becoming the best ME! Without feeding and growing and nurturing me, I could NOT live and give the best to others. I had been selfish is asking Why to others. My life is not ABOUT others, but I believe it is FOR others.

It's funny I never questioned, why was I saved? Why did I get found in time and brought back to health? I just moved on. I learned something in my subconscious that day, I think. I learned that it all starts with me. When I am happy, those around me find happiness. I have tested this many times since that day and it's true! It works! I make you happy. I do! This was my purpose. My gift. I found it.

From that point I became the person I am supposed to be. I reached out and admitted I knew very little about what made me, me. Who was I? Why was I judging myself when I adamantly refused to ever judge another? I went on a journey, of sorts, to find out what "I" liked! I brought "me" into focus, which I had never done before. Finally realizing I like me. I love me! I make a difference! I have Worth!
My story is about going from the Blues to finding the Gold hues in life. From feeling worthless and depressed to realizing that I matter – I have worth. My belief is, we ALL have gifts that others need. We exist to make each of us better souls. We must practice self-care and focus on developing ourselves to be the best we can be, so that our "gifts" are nurtured and strengthened. And only then will we have the courage to step forward into the light and share them and be the inspiration and motivation to make this world a better place for all.

My hope is that in reading this piece of my story, some of you may relate and understand this journey. Starting in the Gray of life and working your way thru the colors of life to finding your own Gold hue. I know now that we all must make our own personal journeys, that we must understand and be patient with the lessons on the path we take. I do not feel regret for anything because it has led me here, to be the best me that I can be but I am by no means done. Continuing my travels, taking the dips as well as the triumphs and enjoying the adventures along the way will all feed my soul until I slide into the Finish Line screeching that famous line, "Awesome, Let's do that Again!"

I am a Multipreneur, an owner of multiple small businesses. As a Viridian Energy Associate I educate people on their right to choose their energy supply; As an Uber Driver I help people get where they want to go safely and have a good time doing it; As a Real Estate Investor I turn regular houses into warm, welcoming places for people to call home. And now as an Author I hope to inspire and motivate people to face their fears. To know that others have traveled this path and have come out the other side. Some, like myself, are better people from enduring the struggle.

I have a passion for people and their stories which draws me to do what I do. The jobs I've had, the places I've lived, the goals I follow, the dreams I have for my future, are all surrounded by my love for helping others. I am a Master Networker and meet people on purpose. I love to hear their stories. My talent is caring. My best days are when I have helped another person. Volunteering isn't an afterthought for me, it's my primary reason for getting up every day. When I was a child and was asked, "What do you want to be when you grow up?" I always answered, "Everything, just once!"

My history is indicative of this very goal. My resume reads like a book. It's been said I should write a list of what I haven't done – that it would be shorter! I don't believe I am struggling to find my "true calling", I believe that trying everything, meeting as many people as I can, helping where I can, experiencing, living, my adventures, are EXACTLY what

I'm supposed to be doing. My grace is in the living, the trying, and the learning.

I grew up in The Berkshires of Massachusetts, and moved around a lot, Hawaii, Wisconsin, Vermont, landing in Worcester, MA where I met the love of my life. We recently moved to Texas and currently live in the Dallas/Fort Worth area. Besides helping others, I love to travel, learn about anything historical, and taking pictures of nature and architecture. I've never met a stranger and would always help anyone who asked.

# Sharon Gulley

**MY JOURNEY TO FREEDOM**

I was seventeen at the time and I was living in Georgia, where his family lived and his three children, and ex-wife. My then husband had been offered a job on an Oil Rig in Oklahoma and I was looking forward to seeing Oklahoma for I had heard so much about the lakes and rodeos that were there. We had been married for about a year or so then and yes, I married very young. Something else I should have thought long and hard about before doing it. We had lost everything we had in Texas to his sister who took the deed to our home and put it in her name. So we tried to leave Texas with a broken down car and what few clothes we had. The car refused to be fixed so we headed to Georgia on foot. It took us four days to get there with the help of people who offered us rides. We were in Georgia for about 3 months when a job offer came about and I was by then ready to go somewhere, where there was peace. There was way too much hurt and betrayal to ever think we would make it there.

With no way to ever return home or having nowhere to go, I thought maybe this change could help our damaged marriage. I didn't love him the way I should for I could not trust him after so many physical altercations and catching him with his ex or in bed with his ex-wife time and time again, but I was determined to make it work one way or the other or at least until I could find a way to support myself on my own.

His friend drove down from Oklahoma and picked us up and the three of us headed back to Oklahoma where he lived and worked, but when we got there we found out we had no place to stay. Come to find out my husband's friend was living with another family and they did not even know I was coming with my husband. It was meant for my husband to come only and he never told me that. I thought to myself, well that would explain why his friend had such an attitude with me and he does not even know me or have a reason to be angry with me, but I later figured out he wasn't angry with me, he was angry with my husband for bringing me along when he knew I was never meant to be there or that was the plan they had put in place.

This was just one of the long series of betrayals that was yet to come. With nowhere to stay we all decided to go to the job site and see if the job was still in place. We drove for three and a half hours to the job site, it was a long ride out to the middle of no man's land and very secluded. It sat in the middle of a cow pasture a mile from the main road coming into the site. The job was still there for them and for that I was thankful for we only had a few dollars left to get by on until my husband received a check, but there was no place to stay while on the job site. Most everyone there had their own small R.V. or tent to accommodate their selves while on the job.

I felt sick at my stomach with trying to figure out what we could do in the mean time for a place to stay but with being almost broke and being in the middle of nowhere, there wasn't much hope to solving this problem, so we decided to stay in the car until we got paid and then we could rent a place to live. I was worried sick and I prayed for God to give me strength to make the best of a very bad situation and make it better every way I could. I should have stayed behind and if I knew what was coming in the end, I would have. They worked nights while I slept and I explored the massive cow fields for water while they slept during the days. With there being no civilization for miles and miles, water was something we had not much of. Thank God for the peanut butter and light bread we had left over which wasn't much but I was thankful. On the third day I found a cow's watering barrel that was silver and very large, and full of cold water. I headed back to the car just in time for the guys to get up and get ready for work and I made them some sandwiches to eat and I told them about the water I had found, and asked them if they could get a five-gallon bucket from the job site so that I could wash us some clothes and purify some drinking water for us. My husband said sure but you need to watch for rattle snakes out there for there are more of them than there are cows out there.

I said, okay and later that night while on break he brought a bucket to me and asked if I was okay. Sure I am alright but I do wish this could have been a little better for us when it comes to having a place to stay. He looked at me and said you are never satisfied are you? That is not what I meant, I said. I just mean it must be hard working all night like that and not being able to shower or eat a decent meal or have a place to comfortably sleep, that is all I meant. Well you don't worry about me, just worry about yourself, okay. Okay, I replied. He left and went back to work.

 I left a little before daylight the next morning before they got off and headed to the water barrel. I washed up some clothes with the bucket or at least rinsed as good as they could be, washed the bucket and carried back some water to boil. I laid the clothes out on the car to dry and built a small fire and boiled some water to purify it and then I strained it through a T-shirt into a cooler we had in the car while they slept.  It gave us a couple of gallons of water.  The evening started setting in and it was time for them to go back to work and I made their sandwiches for them.  We get off early in the morning and maybe even get paid, Boss said he was going to try and pay us early so we can find a place to live, my husband said to me. That is wonderful then, isn't God good, I asked? He turned and walked away, shaking his head. I was raised with knowing if you need help, call upon him and his angels, he will bring you light and I had been praying for the lord to help us and I felt that he was. The clothes slowly dried before complete darkness set into the red hues of the Oklahoma sunset. I watched the sun go down as I folded up the clothes and placed them in the trunk of the car in our bags. I was hopeful that tomorrow would set us on a good path and things would finally be good for us. I fell asleep in the back car seat thinking of what we might find tomorrow.

I woke up before dawn from the sound of the guys throwing things in the trunk of the car. I sat up and looked out the side window and seen them talking low. I got out and said well, good morning. You are up early, my husband said. I guess the sound of tools will do that for you and I laughed. He laughed back and said, well we got paid and it is a nice check too. I smiled at him and said we can go find a place now, right? Yes, we can and as soon as we can clean up. Where is that water barrel at, you mentioned? Go straight out about 200 feet and look down, it is there on the slope. They both walked off talking like school girls in a low voice. I never thought anything of it.

They had known each other for years. Before they got back, I had everything ready for travel and ready to go. I could see them coming from a distance so I went ahead and started walking to the portable toilet before hitting the road. I got to the door of it just as they reached the car. I waved at him and he waved back. I went on inside and I was there about a minute and I heard the car start. I figured they were checking the oil in the car or water. I finished up and came out the door just to see they had left me. I was shocked for a moment and then I thought well, maybe they are going to cash it and they will be back. I just refused to believe he would just up and leave me like that, but he did. I waited all day and into the next morning, but no one returned for me.

I walked over to the Oil Rig when the sun came fully up and asked for their boss and he came out to talk to me. Hi sir, I don't mean to bother you but I was wondering if the guys have to work tonight or not, I asked. No and they won't ever work for me again as far as I am concerned I hope they never come back. I fired them this morning with pay, He replied.

All I could do is just look at him as if I was lost in a tunnel. Are you okay, mam? No I don't think I am, I replied. Why are you here anyways, he asked? They told me you paid them early and let them off early so we could find a place to live, I told him. Well I am sorry they lied to you, he replied. Yeah and they left me too, I said. I started to cry right in front of this man and bless his heart all he could do is say please calm down. I am sorry but all I know is that I am in Oklahoma, I sobbed. Well we will figure out a way for you to get a ride into town so that you can call someone, okay, he said. Thank you so much and I appreciate it, I replied.

About an hour later he came out and got into his truck and drove over, and picked me up. He took me to town and wished me luck as he drove away. I was just thankful to be off that jobsite. With no one to call for help I started walking out of Woodward, Oklahoma heading south to Georgia to see if that was where he returned to. It started to snow really hard that evening and I was freezing to death with no shoes and only his coat, but I kept walking. I was determined to find out why he would do that to me.

It was such a long and dark highway at night walking and I came upon a very quiet place where you could hear everything. I heard some men laughing and drinking, and I heard music playing. It scared me so much. I knew I was out there alone and did not know how they would react to seeing a 17-year-old out walking this long, dark highway alone. I started to cry and then I kneeled on the highway and began to pray. Somehow I lost time through it all for it was dark when I started praying and when I lifted my head from prayer it was daylight and the first thing I seen was a couple of cows under a windmill drinking water and I began to praise God and laugh at myself. I knew that day that God was going to be with me all my life and I never needed to doubt his love and grace.

I made it to Weatherford late that night. I was about 10:30pm. I walked into the Police Station and asked if I could sit in the Lobby until daylight. I was greeted with a big No! Shamefully I threatened to break a window in order to have a warm and safe place to stay if necessary. The Police officer seen me crying and seen I had no shoes on my feet and relented long enough to get help for me so I could have a place to stay.

He called a Social Worker out of Oklahoma City, Oklahoma and she drove a long distance to pick me up, but bless her heart, she came to get me. We got to Oklahoma City about 12:30 or 1am in the morning and she got me settled into a room at the massive Salvation Army they had there in the city. I was locked in my room for they believed I was a run away. They could not believe I was married or that my husband at the time would run off and leave me the way he did. I spent almost a week there with them running back ground checks on me to verify who I was and if I was telling the truth or not.

 Monday morning came and the Social Worker came to me and cried and said I am so sorry that you had to endure his cruelty and for not believing you, but you are so young and I just can't imagine you being in this situation. We have bought you a bus ticket back to Georgia, but if back to him is where you are heading. I would think long and hard about that, you deserve better and then she hugged me. She brought me some warm clothes and shoes. I thanked her and gathered his jacket I had and she took me to the bus station after breakfast.

 I made it to Georgia only to find him with his ex-wife again and the rest is history; but I learned the highways and became a truck driver so I would never be lost again and my faith in God is stronger now than it has ever been. God placed his angels into my life when I needed them most and I know that he always has an open telephone line into heaven for me. There is never a busy signal and his love and protection is all I will ever need.

Sharon Gulley has been writing professionally since 2005 and has been a professional truck driver and heavy equipment operator until 2010 when she retired to become a fulltime caretaker for her Mother who has Dementia. She holds a class A CDL and is a native of Rhode Island. As the oldest daughter of a Navy family her love for writing and telling short stories began as a child while traveling with her family, but she really became serious about writing and becoming a published author at the age of 48.

Her favorite Authors include, James Agee, Robert Frost, Ann Rice and Emily Dickerson as well as Mark Twain. Moving back to her Father's native state of Florida; She now resides in Jacksonville. Her work can be seen and read on Poetrysoup.com. She is also the Author of (The Butterfly Flutters by).

# Joy S. Pedersen

**FROM FEAR TO FAITH**

All memory from the beginning of time is stored within your subconscious mind. The subconscious mind is also referred to as your inner child. That aspect of you is your memory bank and computer. It not only stores your memories but it projects out into the world your beliefs of yourself, others and the world.

If you are not experiencing preferred results and life experiences, the answers often lie within your subconscious. By accessing what is hidden within your memory bank, you can then determine that which serves you or not. All of life is a mirror. By noticing what is going on that you find less than preferable, including undesirable feelings and experiences, you know there is an aspect of that within a story in your mind. By looking within, and letting go of that which does not serve you, you can set yourself free from any and all limitations.

I made this discovery when working at Paramount Studios in Hollywood. While I found it relatively easy to get a job doing television publicity there, others reached out to me for assistance so they could find their ideal job at the Studio. It caused me to want to find out what set me apart. Why was it easy for me and more difficult for them? I found out about the Law of Attraction learning that like attracts like. I then intentionally set my mind to attract what I wanted with success. I realized it was easier for me to break into Hollywood than it was for others because I was naive of the common belief that 'it is hard to break into Hollywood'. Fortunately, I didn't have that self-limiting belief.

I wanted to help alleviate some of the struggle others were experiencing and began teaching the Law of Attraction. And, although we all had success, we each seemed to have an area where we struggled more in the process of our efforts to manifest. It was obvious that we each had within us some kind of block. That realization sent me down a new path to discover a solution to identifying and releasing those blocks.

I was lead to a Hawaiian spiritual healing process called, ho'oponopono, which meant to correct an error. It was during those studies that I began to learn about the subconscious mind, the inner child. I began working on myself to help myself release the cause of any limiting beliefs and fears that I had within. The more I cleared doing using this process, the freer I became. I went from limiting beliefs about money and fears of not enough, to more freedom around the whole subject of money.

I learned that God was the source of all including my money. I worked on clearing issues I had with God, including any guilt and separation The more I worked on my connection to God, the more easily money came to me.

In 2004, Archangel Michael came to me asking me to change my business model to help others identify and clear the hidden causes of their challenges. During our work together, I came to learn how much outside influences had also sabotaged our success. Many of the causes of our fears and limiting beliefs had been generated by the darkness that existed beyond the visible. Lifetimes of rules, oppression, martyrdom and persecution were culprits as they also provided many negative memories that still existed within our subconscious. They were, unfortunately, also still wreaking havoc within uses they had become a big part of our programming.

We began identifying those lifetimes and clearing them for others so all were set free from the horrors of the past. Michael began telling me I specialized in persecution and I could see why. So many talented people today were not fulfilling their calling because of subconscious fears of persecution from memories long buried within. If you were hanged in another life for being different, your mind would recognize opportunities to get yourself out in the marketplace as threatening and sabotage your results to avoid being harmed again. Memories such as these were causing many gifted people from helping others and making the money they desired.

When you think of how much the world has been set up around rules to serve someone else's preferences rather than your own, you have lived a rather oppressed existence for lifetimes. That oppression often consisted of persecution, martyrdom and punishment of some sort when you didn't adhere to the preferences and rules of others. Those memories are still operating in the background regardless of your awareness of their existence or belief in reincarnation. I have identified many lifetimes for people where were not necessarily convinced they had a past life but were set free to experience life more fully after clearing them.

When Archangel Michael asked me to write his book, I agreed immediately. I had already been doing a form of channeling called automatic writing where messages from God, angels or others came through me from others to the paper rather effortlessly. Unfortunately, I was unwilling to tell anyone else about the book. I was afraid of what people would think of me if I told them I spoke to angels. As you can see, that is no longer an issue. As I looked within, I saw countless lifetimes of persecution I needed to clear. I had been hanged, imprisoned, burned at the stake, etc. It is rather obvious why I didn't want to repeat those experiences. So to keep myself safe, I had no voice. No matter how much I may have wanted to communicate this information, the words would not formulate. I found, however, the more I cleared, the more effortlessly I began sharing my information.

Even after we published, "Wisdom of the Guardian: Treasures from Archangel Michael to Change Your Life", I experienced limited results. It drove me to identify and clear eight more lifetimes that combined memories of persecution, public appearances, and also being published. Anything negative within those lifetimes, became reasons my subconscious did not want me to duplicate these experiences. Fortunately, as I cleared them, I became more fearless.

I have since learned that if I notice myself doing busy work or am easily distracted by others, that there is fear I have within that is sabotaging optimal results. The quicker I became at identifying that was the case, as well as those fears operating in the background, and cleared them using my spiritual healing gifts, the faster I would change my outer results.

I was grateful for this discovery and self-awareness. It became easier and easier to demonstrate the life I preferred experiencing. The more I also worked on my relationship to God, the easier life became overall as well.

I learned that often when I had prayed, did affirmations or set intentions, there were inconsistent results. I was fortunately able to identify that the former teachings I had of God, and especially those that created fear of God, caused blocks in my ability to receive the intended results. I realized that both for my clients as well as for myself, the separation we had from God was what caused the problems. By working on the relationship with God, the results dramatically shifted.

I remembered in my 20s feeling called to serve God but had the limiting belief that in doing so I would be broke and suffer. I also had fear due to the story in the Bible of Abraham being tested asking him to sacrifice his son Isaac. If God could ask that of someone, what would he ask me? Fortunately, I was able to clear my limiting belief, as well as that fear, to do the work I was called to do this lifetime, which was to clear the cause of darkness and heal the karma created by the fallen angels. During that work, it was identified that the story of Abraham was not fully accurate. It had been Satan who was testing Abraham and not God. God said to me that he knew Abraham's heart and did not have to test him. As I have shared that story with others, many admitted to that story not making sense and that they too held that same concern I had.

Darkness had often manipulated our connection to God by teaching fear and fear of God. That separation from God alone caused many to have the feeling of not being good enough. God lies within each of us. By connecting to that significant source within, we become most powerful. If your computer is not connected to the power source, it does not operate optimally. By clearing all the separation from God and cementing that relationship, miracles do happen.

I have found that I have gone from fear to faith with that most powerful connection intact. I hear God speak to me, direct me and provide me with information, as well as love, that goes beyond the imaginable. I am most grateful and confident being able to fully self-express and experience life that is effortless.

Self-discovery took on such depth over the years because I not only learned who I am but I learned of my true connection to the world. I learned how powerful I really am and that was largely due to letting go of fear and connecting to the most powerful source within to express myself fully.

I have learned that if there is something I don't like on the outside, I have the resources within to identify and solve the issue. Here are some of the aspects and steps I take:

1. I check with my inner child (my subconscious memory bank and computer - the part of me that manifests) and ask her what is going on. For example, my clients usually just flow to me naturally. There was two-week period that my business slowed substantially so I asked her (your inner child is always the same gender as your physical gender) what was going on. She responded that I had chosen to go on a diet and deprive her of ice cream. When I told her I would get her ice cream, she immediately told me to call a friend/client, who then announced upon my calling, that she wanted a session). Business turned around immediately and was never an issue again.
2. I have learned to work with my high self as well. My high self is considered my super conscious and the part that remains in heaven most connected to Source God. I have learned to gain expert advice and guidance from her, as she sees the big picture. I have also learned that the more I allow her to operate within me, the more confident, powerful and clear I am.
3. Surrendering to God was not easy for me. I had to identify and let go of much fear before allowing myself to completely surrender to God. When I have learned to allow God to run the show, divine order was able to flow through my life and it became more effortless. If a fear comes up, I can stop that flow immediately. Learning the kind of trust needed to live in divine flow, did not come overnight. But, when I allow it, life couldn't be more sweet.
4. Learning to live in the moment is key. I went from living in my head, out of the past and worrying about the future to living in the moment. My life is now moment by moment. I am present in the moment so I can recognize divine guidance and now take inspired action because I

no longer have fear and have faith in the guidance received.
5. Anytime a fear, disruption, or something out of balance appears, I know the priority is to bring myself back to center, identify and clear the cause, let go of the fear and restore myself to oneness with Source God. Upon doing so, all is restored to balance and divine flow continues.

Looking at the self, taking 100% responsibility for the outcomes and experiences in life, isn't always easy. I know it is easier for me to do this for clients than for myself. When I do for myself, I have to get into the pain itself to release it at times. But, if I am not willing to look at myself, nothing changes.

I often get the questions, "how do we stop the suffering going on, change the world, or create peace, etc." My response is always the same and that is to change the world, you have to change the self. If you want peace in the world, you must establish peace within first.

True safety comes from within. When you have eliminated the negative memories that cause fear, you don't attract fearful situations. It is the fearful memories within that establish the programming that attracts the experiences demonstrated in life. True safety also is that inner connection to Source God. Once you feel safe and trust and learn that if you live in the moment, following divine guidance, you will be making fewer mistakes and living your highest and best potential. Life becomes effortless and fearless.

Joy S, Pedersen is a best-selling author, a Doctor of Divinity, non-denominational ordained minister, Licensed Spiritual Healer and Certified Spiritual Health Coach and the Founder and President of the Holistic Chamber of Commerce of Lakeland and Express Success, the company she founded while working at Paramount Pictures Corporation when in Television Publicity that she transitioned into her spiritual healing practice. Her books "Clear Your Past and Change

Your Future" and "Wisdom of the Guardian: Treasures from Archangel Michael to Change Your Life" as well as blog showcase her channeled messages from God, angels and others to help you navigate and improve life today. You can read more about Dr. Pedersen at her site, www.ExpressSuccess.net and receive free gifts at www.ExpressSuccess.net/gifts.

# Robyn Vintiner

**From Rags to the Riches of Emotional Intelligence**

"Are any of you feeling fear?" I heard myself blurting out. They all turned to look at me and almost as one said, "No. We're excited!"

I had earned the right to be in this gathering of network marketers, but I still felt like a fraud. Sure I had a lot of people who had signed up, but no one was doing anything with their precious registration, the money they had spent to enrol with me. I offered to help these people but "the timing wasn't right, something had cropped up," – the usual excuses. Until this moment in time I hadn't been aware of fear the way it was then. It gripped me and seemed to be present in my life most of the time. I woke with it and went into a fitful sleep at night with it, tossing and turning. Up until that point in my life, things had pretty much gone along as expected. I worked hard and things turned out.

All that changed when my husband died. I realised how I had relied on him to make the decisions that we had already discussed. So here I was on my own, really not feeling like I had control over my life any more. I lost confidence in myself and now I was selling, my least favourite thing to do in the world!

The fear didn't seem to be about anything in particular. You know what it's like when you have an exam or have to speak in public, then when it's over you get back to normal? That's what I had understood fear to mean. The other words I used were anxiety, panic attacks and after a time of this, it became depression. I reached a point where I didn't want to get out of bed. I didn't get low enough to contemplate suicide, but I really wasn't that interested in living, even though I have 3 wonderful adult daughters. I'm not one for drugs, so I started looking for alternatives.

I looked for supplements that I could put in my mouth that would stop my churning stomach.
I read some books all around the topic of fear, and what the letters stood for. I learned that fear and excitement release the same chemicals in our bodies. I had been brought up with the saying, "Don't get too excited it might never happen, so my subconscious wasn't going to take me to the excitement. I learned that when we are fearful we don't use the part of the brain that learns things and makes good decisions. I made some 'bad' decisions that took me a long time to sort out.

This led me to believe I was a failure. Thirdly I learned that those same chemicals, adrenaline and cortisol, are released whenever we feel stressed. No wonder my body was a jittery wreck. One book I read, stood out, and intellectually I identified with what the writer was saying. I felt some hope that I didn't have to stay in this place of uncertainty, indecision and depression.

I went to different healers and one of them used Emotional Freedom Technique (EFT) with me, and slowly I started to turn the ship around. She introduced me to the ideas from 'The Secret, 'and what I heard in there, shifted my focus onto what things I could do for myself. From 'The Secret,' I identified with one of the speakers and bought some material of his. There he was, talking about the consultancy/coaching programmes he had, and the seed was sown. It seemed a huge step to go to the US from New Zealand, to do this training. But after more sleepless nights and ramped up fear, I made the decision to go! This time it was a decision that started me on the path to healing.

Although it's scary to think I am responsible for everything that happens in my life it is also empowering to think I can change whatever I want. I don't have to wait for someone else to do that for me. I don't have to be a victim. I don't have to allow the churned up stomach and feeling of helplessness to 'rule the roost.'

The trip to the US was just the start. I learnt this technique from here, more tools from there. I learned that my conscious mind is only responsible for about 5% of what is going on for us on a daily basis. Wow! Only 5%. That means the subconscious or unconscious part of our minds is 'cracking the whip.' And that part of our mind stores all our memories, beliefs, self-image and habits that we have acquired over the years. I was on a mission to find out what those beliefs were that were holding me hostage.

I trained to become a coach so I could help others who were going through what I had suffered. This was a great start to get to the part of me that behaved from beliefs I had learned from a very young age. I was fearful of things that caused fear as a pre-schooler. One of the jobs of fear is to keep us safe, both physically and emotionally. We are all doing the best we can to bring our children up to be good little citizens. In doing so we are operating from our parent's conditioning and they in turn are operating from their parent's conditioning. We may have to go back many generations to find the root cause for some of the beliefs that are being passed down. This may feel unsafe to a pre-schooler and subconsciously he/she may choose to protect themselves from the hurt they felt, and it's ongoing.

In our training we had to go through all the 'exercises' that we would take our clients through, so we would know what that feels like when some of this information emerges for the first time. I was on a roll to learn more, to find out how other trainings approached this need to understand ourselves better. I went through trainings to help people in groups, trainings that acknowledge the wisdom our bodies can bring to the table, trainings that look at our spiritual approach to life. As a teenager I had turned my back on organised religion, and in doing so, had shut down my connection to all that is, to the insights that come to us daily from the Universal Intelligence.

This gave me a sense of calm and peace. In traditional Shamanic cultures, it is believed that these symptoms of anxiety, depression, addictions and so on, arise from the loss of connection to our soul. I got that! I became a facilitator of Chakradance™ which uses movement of the body to connect with our inner messages.
In one local training I went to, we were encouraged to take up some sort of meditative practice on a daily basis, even if for only a short time. I had the opportunity to learn meditation many years before that, but the thought of clearing my mind of its chatter, was such a monumental task, that I couldn't possibly manage, so better not to start.

However, I learned about the physiological changes that are the opposite to the stress response, that happen simply by sitting down quietly and focusing on my breathing. Who would have thought that such a simple technique could make such a big difference! And it wasn't just me. Everyone in the class was seeing the benefits in some way. I was hooked. The EFT tapping was a good first aid technique as well. I had seen the benefits when I started the journey to climb out of the dark hole I had got into. I am an acupuncturist so I really understood this technique that uses acupuncture points. I also resonated with the idea that it is enlisting the body and its wisdom.

I focused on things that I could do for myself so that I wasn't reliant on making an appointment for this healer or that coach every week. Having healers and coaches has been instrumental in my journey but I wanted to have things I could do at home as well. Of course this does mean I have to be motivated, that I have to engage the conscious mind when the subconscious is screaming, 'NO!' It likes to maintain the status quo because that is where it feels safe.

I learned to talk to the parts of me that are anxious and fearful. It sounded a bit weird at first but I understood that our psyche is made up of all these parts, who make up who we all are. Because of our beliefs, some are shut away so the world can't see them, but others are given a free reign. I found that these parts have a lot of wisdom and have been created in our past to keep us safe and protect us from more hurt.

If they came into being because of something that happened when we were 3, for instance, they continue to believe the threats are, as they were back then. Having a conversation helps them to see that I'm an adult now, and that these things are not the threat they were back then.
It is also useful to understand that because of our upbringing we all have different viewpoints, on what behaviours are, or are not acceptable. The behaviours we have been brought up to believe are unacceptable, stay in our shadow. We don't want others to see we have the ability to behave in a way that is unacceptable! We may not even know that these shadows exist, but if you find yourself reacting to someone else's behaviour, this may give you a clue as to what you are trying to hide.

As a 55-year-old I could remember vividly an incident that happened as a 7-year-old. I felt shame around what I had done regarding a wonderful teacher I had. I had the opportunity to meet up with her as the 55-year-old and I felt sick at the thought of crossing paths again. But I'm an adult, right! I felt the need to apologise and do you know what, you guessed it, she didn't even remember. What I had been brought up to believe was unacceptable was a non-event in her upbringing. What a waste of energy that had been, holding on to that all those years.

All this searching and learning may sound like a huge task. You might think it will be better not to attempt to address it at all. I have an insatiable thirst for learning so I have probably done a lot more than I needed. I also needed to feel that I was competent to help others who seek my help. Once you find a technique or tool that helps you, that may be all you need to do to recognise why the fear is cropping up now, and how you can keep it under control. Fear is a very important message to stop us doing foolhardy things. But we don't want it to paralyse us. We can't turn it off all together, so we need to recognise how it is actually helping us, and it may in fact be a signal that we are stepping out into something new that we really want. If we didn't feel so attached to it, the fear would probably stay in the background.

Life is a journey, as they say. In the last 13 years I have had my foot down hard on the gas pedal. Although I can get the speed wobbles from time to time, I am committed to moving forward in a conscious way, releasing the pressure on the pedal every now and then when it all seems a bit much, but pushing it down hard with excitement at other times as I feel the fear has lost its grip. I wish you all the same anticipation of what is ahead!

Robyn was born in New Zealand just after the Second World War, with the beliefs that young women should be 'seen and not heard.' In fact, possibly not even seen! She also remembers being told that she was too sensitive as though it was a bad thing. Conflicting messages! Her father had survived as a bomber pilot and her mother had survived a childhood that had left emotional scars. They had come through the Depression with a lack and scarcity mentality which is still evident in their lives today, as they make their way through their 90s. Robyn was brought up with strong ethics that were both good and also limiting. She was brought up believing that she had to work hard for everything and did so throughout her schooling and this continues to this day.

There were no major emotional traumas, just the usual throw way comments from parents, intent on doing their best. She played every sport her school had to offer, plus out of school sport like skiing. She wonders now whether this was a legitimate way of having fun and being noisy. Of course there is always a risk of injuries when you play so much sport. A couple of major ones impacted her emotionally, which now gives her an understanding of how this affects her patients healing, and how important it is to address this, as she has done.

She started her working life as a physiotherapist which she still enjoys to this day. It is the connection with people that is her reason for living. She subsequently learnt to add acupuncture to her skills. Although these were both based more on the physical, patients would invariably discuss the emotional things going on their lives. Once she needed help for her own emotional health she realised how helpful this would be for those whose health also needed other things than the physical. She has found that her purpose now is to help her clients in a different way, as an Emotional Intelligent Coach. She feels humbled to walk alongside and support people who are on their journey of self-discovery.
Robyn can be found at www.rejuvenatelife.co.nz

# OLGA GONZALEZ

**THIS IS MY JOURNEY**

As I begin to share my story in these few pages, I pray that you will find the root to your situation, addiction or stronghold that has kept you in the cycle you're in.

My story begins at the age of five. My mom had come to salvation and my father was totally against Christian churches, and if you could only imagine the battle that hit my home as mom announced her declaration to her Lord Jesus Christ. From that day fear was introduced to me, by the raging anger that was demonstrated by my father. He would get drunk and verbally and physically attack my mother, through breaking and throwing everything in sight.
my mom began attending a church regularly and without fail, even suggesting more services by adding morning prayer throughout the week. Not so many eager women to be at church to pray early in the morning but, my mom had found her first love, her true love and a real love she had never experienced before.

I am the youngest of six children so I did not have any place to be but with the only love I knew, my mother. As we begin attending church regularly, the pastor of the church immediately begins grooming me for his own personal use, of his sexual perversion. Within months I became his victim. Every service, every week without fail I was being traumatized. I begin to experienced fear at church, fear at home and by the time I realized, I was living in fear twenty-four hours a day. Fear became my companion. Don't remember a day in my life that I live without fear or recall me feeling safe.

Being happy or at peace didn't exist within me. Even though my father wasn't a Christian man and decided to rage war against my mother's new beliefs, he had some good qualities and was a good man. He taught us, let your yes be a yes and your no be a no, regardless what comes your way. He was and still is a man that believed presentation is everything, always dressed like he was attending a wedding, whether he worked indoors or outdoors. He believed hard work was a requirement of anything you set your mind to do.

Both my parents could have gotten masters in servanthood. They could host people at their home as little as two people and as plenty as forty and over, and treat you like royalty even though a few minutes before guests arriving, there was a great amount of tension, yelling and things being thrown by my father. So with all that being said, I knew had to fake a smile, pretend everything was good and go through the mechanics of life.

I had been trained and learned not to let my feeling or emotions dictate my duties, chores or appearances while out in public or even at home.

The abuse at church continued until I was 15 or 16 years old. My dad's anger increased and continued as my mom's personal relationship with God grew. I began being targeted by my dad for standing up for my mother and defending her. The ingredients needed to raise a healthy child had been invaded by the devil himself and with no one to talk to or confide in, it caused a downward spiral of bad choice after bad choice to the point of attempting suicide once and thoughts of suicide that would regularly visit my mind. By the time I was 19 years old I had seen and done just about everything you could think of.

You're probably wondering where was God in my life in all this. Well to make it plain and simple, as fearful and full of sin my life was, I couldn't run from the facts that existed in my life. First fact, Christian people are as scary as non-saved Christians. Second fact, I saw the power of God numerous of times through my mother and how God would use her, so I couldn't deny his existence. I physically had seen angels and demons through a time my mother had gone to visit my grandfather in Mexico.

My aunt had gone to a witch and God revealed to my mom while we were outside sleeping in the outdoors, what they had brought in the house. I saw in the sky the biggest angel you could possibly imagine slicing demons in half. Out of my mom's open bible in Psalm91, the scripture that says, A thousand should fall by your side and ten thousand at your right hand but it will not come near you, was lighted up and beaming towards the sky where I saw the battle going on. A war was raging within me that the God that my mom served was definitely more powerful but somehow I was not qualified to be loved. My experiences had me believed there was no hope for me.

I began attending a community college to see if maybe my dad would be proud of me. He bragged about my brothers and sisters from time to time, not that he wasn't hard with them as well, but they were gifted in many areas, and I still was seeking for a male's approval and affection. As I began going to school, immediately I met a guy totally the opposite of what I would consider getting serious with and to be honest he had baby mama drama and a wife that was becoming an ex as he was trying to ask me out. Something about his face would not let me lose my focus on him. I agree to go out and on the first date, something within me said, he's going to be my husband and he don't even know it. I was right, we got engaged immediately and began planning our wedding. I finally met someone that I could trust, to tell everything I had buried as a child until present time with him. I almost wanted to sabotage my relationship because I couldn't phantom his love towards me. To my surprise he loved me more. My mom was to me until her death, the example of a God fearing woman, a prayer warrior and Gods voice to me. When she met my husband, she cried and cried. I was getting worried and I ask her please tell me, why are you crying? Her response was, you have needed love and need love and I have prayed for God to send you a man. He's the one and I'm crying because you're going to love him so much, you're not going to come visit me. I never told my mom about my abuse but she always said things to me like she knew something and wanting me to say something to her.

Let's fast forward to when God begin to heal my wounds, he started with the abuse of my childhood, he begins to deal with me, to let it go, stop replaying your memory of all your past hurts. I can't heal you, if you don't surrender it to me. I was married to a good man and I still lived in bondage and in fear. I begin reading scriptures of forgiveness and restoration and the thought of me having children and still going through the same agony was causing me to be in such pain emotionally. I couldn't let myself stay in the prison I was living in my mind. I decided to take God at his word, yes it's a choice that were all given, to believe or not to believe. I chose life and to live it more abundantly. I got on my knees surrendered all of me and begin to ask God to guide me to forgiveness towards the abuser. I prayed with sincerity and with all honesty because he knows all things and he can't fix what you don't give him.

After being in God's presence I woke my husband up and said, we need to talk it serious. He immediately gave me undivided attention. I said, I'm making a decision to forgive and I need you to let me do it. I know you are my hero, my protector, and my safe haven when I'm in fear but the areas of my heart that are wounded can only be healed by God. Please don't be mad because I don't understand the process, I'm choosing to trust God and I know your angry of what I went through but I need your support through this. One thing about my husband to this day, is that he loves me. When I share my heart no matter how hard it is to take in some things, he does listen. He wrestles with his human emotions but he's a God fearing man and always ends up doing the right thing.

I was able to confront my abuser with my husband, my best friend and her husband, two church leaders and the pastor. I couldn't believe the freedom and restoration that begin to happen when he said, I had spoken the truth. He also said, he felt as if he was living in prison, trapped in his own sin and felt liberated as well. He eventually became ill a couple of months later, nothing major but not minor since he was up in age, it was always a concern to his family when he was sick. During the church service, God told me to bless him with twenty dollars, that was a lot for me at the time, it was like telling me to give a hundred dollars.

I obeyed God, you should have seen the look in his eyes of disbelief but he also needed to feel the love of God and that God was a God of restoration. The following day I made homemade fish soup to drop off for him and each time he was shocked at me and I was shocked at what God was doing in me. I had other battles to fight and in the process dealing with family thinking this was about them and not knowing this was about a little girl victimized and wanting to live in freedom and happiness and exchange the clothes of shame to be cloth with the clothes of victory! This is just one of the so many wounds God has healed, there is still so many victories and monuments that I have obtained throughout the years but I felt that all my sins and bad choices of my life started with a root problem, all the other ones were just symptoms of the pain I was feeling.

I don't know what your root is, but I know the God that uplifted the root of bitterness that was in me because of my abuse, he can also uplift yours. The only root I want to spring forth is the root of love and the mercy of God. Let him be your loving father, your judge and     your Prince of Peace. He is a God of justice and the God of restoration and I'm

living proof that if you take God at his word, it will do what it's called out to do.
He who began a good work in you will carry it on to completion until the day of Christ Jesus. Philippians 1:6

My name is Olga Gonzalez, born in Houston Texas, on February 11, 1973. I'm married to Roy Gonzalez and have been for 20 years. We have four amazing children with the potential for greatness, that how we prune them, water them and nourish their lives, is probably one of the hardest assignments God has given us. Our goal as their parents, is that they may find their purpose in which God called them to be and that they may walk in the destiny God has already predestined for them, before the foundation of the world. In Jeremiah 1:5 says, Before I formed you in the womb I knew you before you were born I set you apart.

Both my parents came from Mexico and were only able to finish the sixth grade due to the environment in which they lived in. Children at a young age were put to work and had to help at home with daily tasks that adults face on a daily basis. I'm the youngest of six in my family, there are four girls and twin boys. I pretty much grew up on my own because there's a huge gap between my oldest four siblings and I. My sister next to me was two years older but always stood out in school and had high expectations for herself at a young age unlike me so she attended magnet schools, away from our district. I was always surrounded by family or people in our house but no one that I could relate to or trust on what was going on in my life.

My life began when I met my husband, he was the first person that knew all about me and still never changed the way he saw me. On the contrary he saw strength and potential in a broken little girl and helped me, to see myself, on how God saw me. He was the cheerleader on the stands when no one else sat their besides my mom.

My journey to find my purpose and to find the God that my mom knew, began when my mother died. It was easy to ignore God when you had a praying mom, even when I would have acted like my life was perfect, she would say things like, if you make your bed in the pit of hell, even their God will rescue you. She would say, you can't lie to the holy spirit and my response was, maybe your confusing your children and that word was for one of your other kids. I never understood the function of the holy spirit or really who he was. Heard my mom prayed all my life and yet when she died, I was clueless on how to pray.

I'm thankful to say, I have found my purpose in life, I personally have accepted Jesus Christ as my Lord and Savior and now I know, that the holy spirit is real, he my counselor and he has a voice. He is not a ghost. I have officially opened my ministry, The Sons and Daughters of the King. I counsel and teach people individually and want my ministry to be known for random acts of kindness to all, to the needy and the wealthy. I see my ministry like a clinic, depending on your need, I will help find a solution or try to be the solution to your problem. Success is not carrying a title with great importance, success is living in the purpose God called you to be and having a servants heart in a position of great importance.

You can contact me by email at olga5469@yahoo.com. I am working on getting a website going and getting a number that will be used only for the purposes of the ministry.

# Addie Lamour

**Thriving in Life, Love & Business: My Story.**

While some were born with a silver spoon, I was born with something more special... I was born with a veil over my face. You know what people say about people that are born with a veil over their face- that they have a third eye, a 6th sense? Yeah, that's me.

Growing up, I was always seen as special and not just in my family but just about everywhere else. I was everyone's favorite and was given special treatment. Most times, I felt like the treatment was a little too special. If it was because I was the kid with the cute looks and the attractive and contagious smile or because I was the smart and witty one, I really can't tell, but what I know is my specialness got me into major trouble later on in life.

As a child, I got passed around to a remarkable number of grownups.... People that said I was also their favorite. Most of them loved having a smart and witty kid like me around them and my parents and I would always oblige. I did enjoy the treats that came with visiting older people. While I wish my story could be rosy from the word-go, like most stories you hear, it isn't. On one of my numerous visits to a "trusted grownups' house" the worst thing happened to me. I was molested. While I was really young at the time it happened, I was old enough to know what had been done to me was horribly wrong and I grew up nursing a hatred for men. I had been violated by one of the people that called me special... His favorite. To put it lightly, I felt dirty. I will not reveal the identity of the perpetrator as it's of no relevance to my story. The hatred stayed with me for many years of my life but I somehow managed to move on from all that bitterness and hatred. Life went on...

I remember having dreams as a child, I dreamt things that came to pass. Every morning after waking up, I would walk out of my bedroom and the first thing my family would say would be "good morning" followed by "any dreams you want to share today?". People never joked with my dreams or my interpretations of other people's dreams... Well, neither did I. Of all the dreams I dreamt as a child, few stuck with me. These dreams were so vivid and I remember having them all the time. They were dreams about live flowers and living waters. In my dreams, when I touched the flowers they would move as if they were human, and the water was so beautiful and blue, the water even came alive when I touched it. There were also huge butterflies flying around very low with lights on their wings. Everything was so vivid it was just like seeing a 3D movie. That world was so beautiful and tranquil.... Then I would wake up to real life.

My adolescent and teenage years were pretty uneventful. Aside for puberty and its effects, I can't recall anything worth mentioning. Yes, I went to school like other kids, and did well enough for a regular kid. I made a few friends... Parted ways with them after high school. The truth is I really can't recall being happy as a teenager, I just took each and every single day as it came. I always looked forward to going to sleep just so I could dream my beautiful dreams. That world was a much happier place than my real world... For me the real world was just a blur in comparison with my happy place.

Fast forward to my twenties... Yes, I fell in love and did all that good stuff... Seemingly good at that time. I was born again and supposedly on fire for God but I lacked one thing, discipline and self-control (that's actually two things) I was new with the whole Christian life and was still trying to find a balance between who I was and who I was meant to be. In that short time, I made a lot of wrong decisions and took a lot of wrong turns. All of these led to me getting pregnant somewhere along the line.

Still active in church but this time with a three (3) month old kid, I met this guy in church and fell crazily in love with him. We got married and had two (2) kids. To onlookers and passersby, those who knew us, who saw us in church, at the mall, in the neighborhood and just about everywhere else, we were the perfect family. With three beautiful kids, we seemed like a happy couple... If only they knew. To put it lightly, my life and my home were a living hell. The man I married, the same one I said I loved and who claimed to love me back (well at least in public he did say so and acted as such) beat me at least two to three times a week... Every week of my life.

Just so the kids wouldn't know, these beatings happened indoors... With our bedroom door closed. I would be threatened not to make a sound during the beatings. Our kids were either too young to understand or assumed our quiet fights and arguments were us "playing love" Wondering how I masked the scars and bruises that ensued from the beatings? Well, let's just say I stocked up on make up more often than the average lady of my age. From foundation, to concealer and blushes I had them all. I had done my research on which brands provided the greatest coverage and mastered the act of masking bodily bruises. Needless to say, my face, neck, arms and sometimes my legs got a decent amount of these make up products.

I was willing to do anything- anything to hide my reality from the world, anything to prevent lying that I tripped and fell or hit my face against a door, anything to prevent the world from seeing the man I married for who he truly was. I remember being pregnant with my son, and he beat me with a broom stick. Was he wicked or heartless or was I plain stupid?

For those asking if or why I didn't get out of that house and far away from him... I did, several times too! I ran away a couple of times but he found me and brought me back home, back to him. Did I feel special every single time he begged and pleaded to have me back? Was I just hopeful he wouldn't hit me anymore as he had promised? Was I hoping I would be able to keep from doing the things that made him hit me (which sometimes included simply breathing)?

In retrospect, I really can't tell what kept me in a relationship with a physically and verbally abusive man for 15 beautiful years of my life. One thing I know for sure was I was afraid of him, oh and I did love him... The problem is I didn't love myself. One thing that I can recall was I really had no money to my name. He didn't want me to work and made me dependent upon him. I had no money to get out of the situation or was that just my excuse? Whatever I had would be used up by the time he came begging for me to return. Also, the urge to see my two and later three kids was a major pull for me.

**Thriving in Life...**

At a point in my life, I got tired of asking him for money. When I would be home with the kids, I would look for ways to make money and that was how and when my journey as an entrepreneur began. I taught myself how to use different programs, I started making wedding and birthday invitations, oh yeah, did I tell you I'm very creative. Soon, I purchased a camera and started shooting weddings for people who didn't have the money to hire a professional photographer, I would even help decorate the wedding venue. Any way I could make money legally, I did.

I finally got the courage I needed to file for a divorce. After which he went to jail. But guess what! I remarried him after he got out and the abuse continued, but this time it didn't last for too long. I finally got tired of the way I was living, tired of the empty promises and tired of being treated like a punching bag. I sought for advice and started preparing myself both mentally and financially to leave and this time for good. I finally saved enough money to open my dance studio and enough courage to finally leave. I left him and this time it was final. It was hard and yes he still tried to have me back but my mind was made up. I had moved on from him and I had promised myself never to return to him or look back and it somehow happened. I felt the pain of separation, even though I know he was horrible to me, it didn't make it hurt any less. Some nights I would dream terrible dreams of him beating me, on other nights it would be his voice I heard but I would see a different face. I would wake up sobbing bitterly. This phase of my life didn't last for a long time. After weeks of wetting pillows, I let him go. In my heart and mind, I forgave him and the horrible dreams stopped coming. I was ready to live again and this time I promised myself I would thrive at this thing called life.

**Thriving in Love... Or not?**

Even after the years of hard beatings and bruises, I still looked good. I guess I had a resilient skin, soon I had no need for masking scars as most of them had disappeared and with them, the pain and hurt from my past relationship. I started dating again, I met a few good men every now and then but none had really caught my fancy enough to start something serious. Not until I met this man, everything seemed to be great about him, we had great conversations and we seemed to flow at the same rate, speed and level. We would stay on the phone for hours having meaningful conversations, he was funny and kind. Could this be the one? Could he be the one? After months of consideration, we finally got married! My love life was thriving; my business was thriving... Life was good.... Or so I thought.

I couldn't believe my love life was back on track after two years of leaving Mr. Ex. Then it happened, the new guy, my Mr. nice guy started showing me different angles of him that I never saw before. He was super secretive and a very private person, his cell phone was always locked and close by (not that I really intended picking it up and scrolling through... Or did I?) His private life was really nothing compared to the disappearing acts that he started pulling off. He was pretty much the man of the disappearing acts. He would simply take off for weeks and sometimes months with no warning, no information on where he was going and calls from him would be far and in between. While there was no abuse or proven infidelity, the marriage went sour because of his secretiveness and his unwillingness to make it work and to act like a real husband. During the time I stayed married to him, my business also went down. Business was so bad that I just stopped it altogether for two years. In this time, I lived off my savings and the money he left me with whenever he was around... Did I tell you he was generous too? Well he was. But who needs a generous husband who's never around. I spent 10 years with this guy- it was really an off and on relationship- after which I found myself in another divorce.

**Thriving in Business.**

After the divorce, I opened my business back up, and I'm happy to let you know it is thriving better than ever. I have since opened three more businesses- a daycare center, a fun center and a printing business. I also started a women's empowerment group where I inspire other women in matters relating to life and business. I am a successful entrepreneur who is helping others- men and women alike- to start their business. I am also currently coaching two women in starting their own daycare center.

Sometimes I wonder what changed in me and how come my mindset is now different. I guess the truth is that I have learnt to treat myself as special. All of my life, right from being a toddler, I had gotten used to being seen as special, being given attention and being treated as everyone's favorite, so much that I had forgotten how to see myself as special, give myself attention and be my very own favorite person. Waiting for people to treat me this way made me settle for people who were not deserving of me, and those who never knew my worth. It would start with rude remarks and putdowns here and there that I would tolerate and would later gravitate into slaps, kicks and blows. I was deserving of so much more, I was precious and in need of someone who would understand that and treat me likewise. I deserved to be treated with love and care and not as if I was a punching bag; I needed to be treated like a wife and not a roommate.

Finally figuring my worth did me a lot of good. Today and every day since I understood that I matter, I look into my mirror and remind myself of these... That I'm precious, that I matter, that my feelings matter. that I'm worthy, that I deserve the best and that I don't have to settle.

Today I'm single and loving it. I'm in a growing relationship with the two people that love me the most in this world- my Creator and myself and I'm happy with this. Realizing that I really do not need to be in a relationship to be fulfilled has helped me decide not to settle for anyone who is undeserving of me and my love. I'm currently focusing on growing my businesses, helping others start and grow theirs and building strong relationships with people. If a great guy comes along- one who understands what it means to truly love a treasure like me, I'm in! But until then, I'll focus on being the best version of myself... The one thriving in life, love and business.

The one in love with the person staring right back at her in the mirror... The one in love with me! This is all real... This is my story.

Addie Lamour is a 46-year-old mother of 3, successful entrepreneur. I have 4 successful businesses. My children are Grace 22, Hannah, 25 and David 19. I have 2 adorable grandchildren, Haleigh 2 and Ryan 5.

I am a Life and Business Coach. I love what I do. I love helping others succeed. I love seeing others happy. I own a Pre-school, Dance Studio, Basic Design and Printing Company and I have a Fun Center/Party Place. I am currently writing my own children's entrepreneur book and program that will be taught in schools. I'm simply just enjoying my life at this point and time in my life.

# Anu Mari Holopainen

**The chase that led me to the cross   John 15:16**

As a young child it was not unusual to find me playing outside for an entire day, I absolutely loved the freedom I felt outdoors. Only hunger or thirst could force me back home after venturing around the suburbs with my next door neighbors. They were days filled with imagination and happiness as we searched for secret hidey holes inside thick shrubs and bushes that we claimed as our own territory. We would spend hours exploring and discovering new little worlds to frolic in and create our pretend life to be whatever we wanted.

Those adventurous days were carefree and exciting; it was as if we were the creators of our own kingdoms. In our pretend kingdoms the only opposition we were met with was bad weather or other children that had discovered our secret place demanding it to be theirs. Once the fun stopped for the day and the distractions were gone I was faced with my broken self on the inside.

We each have our own childhood stories and memories that will stay with us forever. It can often take a conscious effort to remember the good parts of our childhoods when the bad parts have come through and almost set fire to everything inside of you.

As I mentioned in my biography school set the scene for a lot of frustration due to the language barrier that I had between me and the rest of the class. While memories of every specific event as a young schoolgirl tend to be forgotten over time, the consequences of those situations that bought intense hurt and pain into my emotional world caused grief into many areas for several years.

As a child it was difficult to comprehend the reason for children laughing and poking fun at me and more than likely it was uncomfortable for those children to be around me as I struggled to communicate, we all know silence can be awkward. My personality wasn't much help to me either. Naturally as a person I am on the introverted side rather than extroverted which tends to put me at the back of the pack so to speak in many settings.

I am not the one to simply stick my hand up in the air and say 'pick me'. Being introverted and having a language barrier meant that being last became second nature. Over time one building block of rejection built upon another and eventually the person left standing was no longer the true me it was the broken me.

My name Anu also added to the rejection that was taking place, young children in those days were not used to different names such as mine. This resulted in my name Anu becoming quite popular in conversation however not in a good way. From primary school through to high school I carried with me a lack of identity and an immense amount of self-hate.

The high school years in general tend to represent an earth shattering and life changing development. Children move up to another level in education and girls in particular experience turmoil as her body begins to transform into a woman, creating a very vulnerable time in any girl's life. The day that I walked into high school is the day that every negative experience in primary school walked in with me. In fact, it didn't just walk in with me it lived inside of me. From the moment I woke up in the morning to when I dropped into bed each day the thoughts that overwhelmed me were dark and oppressive.

To be honest I cannot remember a single day that I felt comfortable in my own skin. My daily routine started with rehearsals in front of the mirror in which I would speak out the words *'I'm so ugly, just so ugly. Why? Am I so ugly, no boy in his right mind is ever going to want me".* There was not a crumb of belief in me that I would ever have a boyfriend, but *Oh* how desperately I craved to be loved by someone. There were nights that I stood at my bedroom window staring into the dark skies lit up by a concert of stars, imagining the impossible, dreaming that there was someone out there who was going to love me.

In our family I was the eldest of four girls, so having no brothers didn't really give me much practice in talking with boys. Any attempts in high school to capture the attention of a boy I secretly had a crush on flopped very quickly. I had no self-esteem, no confidence and could barely muster up a few words in front of a classroom when asked by the teacher to participate in a classroom exercise. Those types of situations were my worst enemy, as there was no hiding the insecurities I felt since my bright hot red face would turn on like a traffic light signaling my embarrassment.

 My heart would pound so hard and fast in my chest that I thought I was going to have a heart attack in front of everyone.

At the end of each day I would replay in my mind everything that had gone wrong. It was as though I had my own 24 hour t.v. channel playing inside my head.  There was no escape from myself and my thoughts. The more time went by and the longer the channel kept playing the more I was consumed with everything that I believed was wrong about me.
The power of those negative thoughts and beliefs were very destructive personally and relationally. So destructive that I could not even hold onto my first boyfriend as I did not

understand what real love was so I pushed it away. I suppose to comprehend that someone actually loved me when I hated myself was so contradictory. After our breakup, my life suddenly turned into the chase.

Having low self-esteem did not stop me from making extra efforts to connect with guys. The emptiness that was consuming me screamed out daily to be filled. To 'not' have a guy in my life was not an option, I had to have someone. I needed to have someone to hold and be held by. This intense desperation to be loved put me into several situations which left me heart broken. So the emptiness and longing continued to multiply. At the time while I was going through this desperate chase for the 'perfect' someone I had no idea how broken I really was. I sold myself with convincing stories for why I should stay with a guy that was clearly using me. It was as though a magnet pulled me towards all the wrong types of guys.

It only makes perfect sense that when you hate yourself it is easier to stay with someone who is hurting you and using you as that is all you believe you are worth. It is almost like another level of hating yourself when allowing another person to hurt you. However, at the time this logic did not enter my mind. The hate that I felt towards myself kept me in prison, locked up with all the wrong types of people. Locked up in self- hate and oppressive thoughts that dictated my decisions and choices in life.

Having been in several relationships although short lived and having completed school, I was working when my life took an unexpected turn. It was just an ordinary day like every other, yet something quite different was starting to unfold. Several ladies I worked with were reading an article which was grabbing their attention until it grabbed mine. Curiosity got me reading the article which was discussing Jesus return. The article was attention grabbing but quite misleading as it declared the exact day and time Jesus was coming back.

Curiosity and worry persuaded me to grab the article and take it home to show my dad. He read it and assured me it was not true, providing me with the evidence from the bible that states clearly "no one knows the day or the hour that he returns". I felt sudden relief at discovering the falseness of what was written yet the idea that there was a Jesus who was coming back didn't want to leave me.

This then lead to another situation at work in which someone had left brochures on the tea room table advertising a Christian event. I felt urged to go and somehow I was so curious about whatever this Jesus, God thing was so I needed to find out. It was in this meeting that all of a sudden my eyes were opened to the knowledge that there was a God and that he loved me unconditionally. That God had loved me even while my life was a mess. This is when the biggest change of my life took place. I committed my life to Jesus and suddenly my life took on some purpose and meaning. No longer was I an empty soul travelling through life desperately searching for love.

While I wish I could say that after I met Jesus my life was miraculously perfect from then on, however it wasn't. The major difference this time around was that I had the love of God in my heart and an assurance that he had me covered. He had called me and made me for a purpose and this gave me so much more than I had ever experienced previously. The need of having a man in my life was no longer a desperate focus; my heart was filled with such amazing acceptance and love from God which gave me a security I had never known of. While in my heart I felt satisfied with single life and was not really looking, I met the man I would marry in the same church. Something about him seemed so familiar and it just drew me to him. To say that I was all fixed up and sorted was not the case, yes I had god's love and forgiveness in my life but little did I know that it was only the beginning of a life of healing and transformation. That I was yet to go on a journey that was hard and heavy which was going to pull me apart and put me back together again.

Becoming a Christian and giving my life to Jesus was the first door I walked through for wholeness. I still carried with me all of the brokenness that had kept me oppressed and enslaved for years. The man that I married and the man I am still married to today also had a lot of brokenness inside of him which meant that our journey was going to be a long and painful process.

In our first year of marriage we lived through what you would call a bad nightmare. We fought and we clashed, it was not a romantic movie scene but rather a war movie. We didn't fight physically but we fought verbally and with the classic silent treatment. The tension was almost unbearable at times and neither of us stood skilled in communication, relationships or successful living for that matter. We made so many mistakes, however we had God on our side who knew us better than we did. He had a plan and the plan is still unfolding to this day.

As I mentioned a few paragraphs earlier I had god in my life yet I was far from being a healthy person on the inside. The 24 hour t.v. channel was still playing inside my head and dictated what I could or couldn't do. Now that I was married all of my insecurities were surfacing on a regular basis. Just a simple trip to the local mall had the potential to change my mood by the time we walked out of there and headed home.

My husband and I had already experienced this while we were engaged however it just intensified after we got married. I felt insecure and ugly so I projected those hurts onto my husband. If my husband even so much as slightly looked in the direction of another woman who looked amazing I reacted with intense and overwhelming fear and pain. I would question my husband like a judge and ask "did you or did you not stare at that woman?". None of his answers bought any comfort as I was so convinced of how ugly and unwanted I was that it did not matter what my husband did or didn't do as I was living out of my brokenness. Brokenness is like an open wound that has not healed so when a suitable scenario takes place it touches that wound and causes immense pain. In those days I did not know how to connect the two together.

I blamed all of my pain on my husband until one day he said to me "the more you keep telling me to not look at other women the more it is making me want to". It had started to have a very negative effect on him but that comment got my attention! For the first time I stopped and thought about what he said and realized that something needed to change or this was going to turn into a major catastrophe.

One night we decided we would go and watch the movie "pretty woman". Throughout the entire movie I was inwardly screaming and crying feeling so ugly and rejected. How could I ever possibly measure up to all the other women who seem so free to be themselves? The idea of being free felt completely impossible. I thought I was going to be stuck with low self- esteem or self -hatred for the rest of my life. It was after this movie in which God was going to speak to me through my young husband and give me a key to my healing.

We had got into the car and began driving home when all of a sudden I could not hold it in any longer and I just burst out into an incredible surge of tears and pain. Why was I like this, why couldn't I be like everyone else and just be happy to be me? It was at that moment my husband pulled over to the side of the dirt road and said "you know what you need to do?", "you need to forgive those that have hurt you, pray and forgive them and ask God to forgive you for your hatred towards those people".  This concept was completely new to me yet so very powerful.

The very first step of forgiving those that had hurt me was a vital key in me being who I am today which is the reason for why I do what I do.  Freedom is available for you too!
Life is not always good to us and our deepest hurts can travel with us until we recognize that we need to let them go.  From

childhood through to adulthood I felt as though I was a prisoner inside my own skin. On the outside I was like every other child and enjoyed playing outside with my neighbors or my three sisters.

On the inside there was a battle that continued to intensify as I got older. There was nothing I liked about myself, in actual fact you could say that 'I hated myself'. Low self-esteem and self-hatred had me bound and unable to live in freedom to enjoy life. This struggle unfolded into small little victories when the one that I had been looking for all along had found me, his name was Jesus.

At the age of five months old my parents and I began a new life in Australia after they had decided to leave our beautiful home country, Finland. Over time the family grew which gave me three lovely sisters. For several years my parents struggled to speak the English language which meant that my only language up until the first day of kindergarten was Finnish. On the first day of school and several months later I felt very detached and frightened, as there was a huge barrier between me and the other children.

Not only was there a language barrier, my name Anu was different it was not what the other children were used to. So sandwiched between being unable to speak the language and having a strange name *plus* being more of an introverted type of personality my schooling days challenged me every day.

It was no surprise that most teacher's descriptions of me in my school reports read "Anu is a shy and quiet girl", which ultimately became my identity it was who I was.  After completing Year 10 in High School 1985, I had no desire for any further study but instead went on to earn my own money as a data entry operator. My life revolved around emotionally surviving from one day to the next as my heart, mind and spirit was broken. This led me to the chase, the chase of finding that 'one man' who I believed was going to fix all of my problems.

The never-ending search had left me feeling more rejected and unwanted until one day I walked into a church meeting and discovered for the first time that there really was a God and he loved me completely. I found my husband in church and we have been married for 27 years with five lovely children. Having God walk by our side however, does not guarantee a life trouble free. In the darkest of times I found it challenging to find someone who I could openly talk with. Which is why I decided; "What the heck I might as well talk about it".  Email: anumaritruebeauty@yahoo.com.au; Website: https://anumariblog.com/

# Francia Noble

**I Am More Than Enough**

I am the fourth child of two very southern parents. Southern in that we were raised to say please and thank you, no matter what. We never met a stranger. And dinner was always served promptly at 5:30, with all of us around the table before grace was said. Southern in how our parents made certain that we went to church every Sunday. Southern, family meant everything. Southern neighbors looking out for each other and sharing fresh raised vegetables from the garden. I was simply a southern girl, who enjoying spending Saturday evening with her father watching the Carol Burnett Show and playing with my favorite doll, Mrs. Beasley modeled from the TV sitcom, Family Affair. I was a happy little girl, and then the unthinkable happened.

Did you know that it is estimated that at least two out of every ten girls and one out of every ten boys are sexually abused by the end of their 13th year? Did you know that most children, who are sexually abused, are abused by a family member or close friend? Did you know that "stranger danger," by comparison, is quite rare? (http://www.childmolestationprevention.org). But I was only 7, why did this happen to me?

It was a summer evening; I recall hearing the roar of the window air conditioner being the only sound in the now empty house. All of the boxes had been loaded into the truck earlier that afternoon. It was with mixed emotions that my family member and her family were moving. For the past few years, it had been pure joy to walk out of my back door, across our yard, into their yard, and then the back door. From all the trips made back and forth, there was a clear wear pattern in the once plush green grass.

Now at the age of 40 plus, there are days that I still ask the question, "why was I there"? How did I come to be alone with him? I plead with my mind to retrieve the answers, yet nothing comes.

All that comes to mind is that the house was cool and clean. I could see the tracks in the carpet left by the vacuum. The small bedroom located on the front of the house had once be occupied by a little girl. The room had a luminous glow from the full moon shining through the uncovered window. Even though the floor is carpeted, in this moment if feels hard to my back and my bottom. I can see the glow-in-the-dark stars' ion the ceiling. At any other time, this would have been a fairy tale setting. I am wearing one of my favorite sailor dresses that had been hand-sewn by my mother; she makes all of my clothes. My underwear is pink with little lace ruffles. I don't remember if he threatened me in any way, or maybe he made me promise not to tell anyone. I can't hear his voice. All I know is that he was there, pulling my princess girl panties down around my ankles. I lay still, not sure what was happening. He had large hands. They felt rough on my legs. It was quiet, no one was coming. I think that was important because he stopped and appeared to be holding his breath. And then he touched me. Hi fingers were moving in and around my "pocketbook". His sweat is dripping on my cheek. What is he doing? Why is he doing it? I did not move. I did not speak.

After what seemed like hours, he wiped my face and pulled up my panties. I was sent back across the yards, walking the trail as I had so many times before. Slowly I walked up the five wooden steps, leading to the door, back into my family home. No one asked what was wrong. No one noticed that I was different. No one noticed that I had just become a statistic of child molestation. I never mentioned the event to anyone and thankfully, it never happened again. I spent the next few years trying never to be alone with him. I could not always avoid being around him, but I knew that I could not allow him to do what he did to me ever again. Sleepovers were torture, since I feared he would touch me again; so I did not sleep. He was always so open with things that should have been private. He would go to the bathroom and leave the door open, knowing that someone may walk by. Once I even saw him taking a bath with the door open. It was as if he wanted people to see his naked body. But by God's grace, I managed to keep out of his grasp until they relocated to another state.

It was many years later that I learned he had also molested another family member. But the bigger lesson came years later as I grew into an adult woman. You see, the mind does not forget. We can suppress memories, but there will always be triggers that bring those memories back to full consciousness.

Over the next few years, my world was crushed even more. A sibling graduated from high school and joined the armed forces (leaving home, until to return on visits). But most devastatingly, my parents got a divorce. My home went from the typical household, to one of being broken and on shaky ground. I moved from private school to public school, as my mother could no longer afford the payments on her own. Or at least that was my thinking, since I was never really given a reason. I walked home most days to an empty house, as my sister was off doing extracurricular activities. I came to enjoy spending that time alone in the house, because no one was there to hear or see my tears. And slowly I began to forget. Trying to become the happy child once again.

I did say memories have triggers; that trigger was his death. Not only did I have to attend the funeral, I was asked to sing. How could I minister in song during the funeral service of the man who had changed my life in such a horrific fashion? I tried to say no, but my family insisted. Of course they would since they had no idea how this person had violated me. The more I insisted that I could not, the angrier they got, particularly my mother. Finally giving in to the "guilt-trip" that she played on me, I agreed. I was about half way through the song when the flashback occurred and the tears began to flow. Naturally, everyone just thought I was overcome with the emotion of the day, if they only knew.

Through my adult years, I have been in and out of relationships. I married at 18 simply to get away from my family. During which time I was blessed with 2 beautiful kids. He wasn't abusive or didn't love me, or so I thought. I was young and did not know how to be married. I simply did not know how to be me. He was killed in a car accident before I ever learned how to be his wife. I re-married again a few years later to a man who was more concerned about pleasing his parents than taking care of our household. To this union, a child was born. I had to leave him when I realized that he had been unfaithful and stopped financially supporting our growing family. It was likely during this time that those suppressed childhood memories began to surface again. You see, I began to think it was me who had the problem. It was me who was messed up and did not know how to love the men that I thought God had blessed me to marry. It was me who did not know how to be a woman. It was me who simply was not good enough. It was me who was the over-weight, nagging, not so great housekeeper who simply did not know how to be a woman, a wife, a mother. In my mind I had become a prisoner to that one traumatic event in my life. I was tainted, damaged goods, unworthy of love and affection from any one, and no one knew. IT WAS ME!

In 2007, my former mother-in-law asked a question about my marriage to her son. We had been divorced for almost 6 moths and she had no idea. He had managed to keep all of those details to himself. To my surprise, he had kept the horrors of our relationship private. No one knew of the sexually transmitted disease he contracted. Yet due to our lack of intimacy, he had not been able to pass it on to me. Thank you God for your protection. In what I believed was her attempt to place blame on me for the marriage failing, she asked, "Was my son such a terrible husband"? To which I calmly replied, "For me, yes he was." It was in that moment that all of the praying and crying came together as one. Clear as if he were sitting next to me, I heard the voice of God say, "I made you and you are more than enough". She and I said our goodbyes and we have not spoken since that day, nor has she had any contact with her granddaughter. And it certainly has not been for a lack of trying on my part. I have replayed her question over and over, and each time God has said, you are more than enough.

Tears flowed down my cheeks as I recalled Psalm 139:14: "I praise you because I am fearfully and wonderfully made; your works are wonderful; I know that full well." I am made in the image of the one who created both the heavens and the earth. No man or women will ever be allowed to have that kind of power over who I am or who I am to be. I choose to live each day as the strong empowered women that God created. It is through his grace and mercy that I have the freedom to stand tall and share a story that has never been told. I am empowered by the presence of other women as we join through stories and hearts filled with love. No matter the circumstances I may find myself. I know that I am loved, I am forgiven, and I AM MORE THAN ENOUGH.

Francia Smalley-Noble is a human behavior expert, author, speaker, and professor who has spent the majority of her career developing individuals across major domains of business and education.

Her primary focus has been on Human Behavior, Organizational Education and Leadership Development within the functional areas of Customer Service, Behavioral Health, and Spiritual Ministry. She is also a business and psychology professor and is the author of **Doing Business God's Way: A Collection of Devotionals for the Entrepreneur.** As a public speaker and facilitator, Francia shares expert insight into the human behavior and is known for interacting with participants – often including participants in her presentations to enhance the learning experience.

Francia's distinctive communication skills set her apart when it comes to effectively inspiring individuals and stimulating teams to pull together in order to accomplish an organization's objectives. Servant Leadership is at the heart of Francia's approach and that is soon recognized as authentic by those who work with her. The result is a bond of trust that creates an environment of growth, value-based relationships, appreciation, accountability and fun.  She is a proponent of talents and gifts that have been developed around one's core belief system, and how they strive to live a purpose driven life. She also subscribes to the ideology that our physical, mental, and spiritual health is as important to maintain, improve and nourish as our professional development.

**Areas of Expertise**
---Effective client relationship building with strong relations and communication skills.
---Extensive knowledge of the social science field; i.e. Psychology  and Human Behavior
---Resilient relationship building abilities; she maintains well-developed interpersonal and networking
skills; and is beyond capable of thriving in both individual

and team settings.
---Extremely attentive to details with an industrious work ethic stemming from years of science and research.
---Passionate about lifelong learning and success. Driven by innate competitiveness and desire to push personal limits. Keeping her grounded is never an easy job, but her 3 bratty kids and dachshund named Bishop T D Jakes (that is another story), handle the task with poise and grace. With them all, she enjoys quiet time at home crocheting and cooking special dishes. Her one bucket list item that she is determined to make happen is to tour the Holy Land.

# Winnie Smith

"UNDERSTANDING THE INEVITABLE; WHEN FEAR MEETS FAITH"
*Now Faith is the substance of things hoped for, the evidence of things not yet seen. (Hebrews 11:1)*

Identifying the fears in my early life, was more of an emotional state, than physical, the fear of GOD ways and will for my life. Seeing Spiritual imaging and experiencing the move of God, because of Gifts been hand down from Generation to generation. Now all of these things was embedded in my "MORTAL BODY" which was natural for me as a child, being very ENTHUSIASTIC: keen, fervent, ardent, passionate, warm, zealous, excited, spirited, exuberant, wholehearted, hearty, committed, devoted, fanatical, earnest: informal, mad about. With so much ENTHUSIACISM: The fierceness, the strength, the perseverance to move forward at any given challenges, not knowing it was the God In me, I had believed from a young age. I would say about 9yrs old witnessing the fig tree during Easter time, and getting the knowledge to cut the tree, and to experience the blood at the hour of 12:00pm Good Friday, the hour of when Jesus was crucified thousand years ago. I remember doing the same again after 12:00pm noon on the same day, and the result was different, clear stany water.

Before we move on, a word of caution is in order. You will not be able to hear God's voice; If you have not surrendered your life to God. I was very young when he started calling me & showing me great spiritual things. When I was trying to get others attention, so they could see, it ain't happening at all. I believe by the spiritual things of God, that I am a "CHOSEN ONE" place here on earth for a specific task, which took me this far to realize the true purpose of my Lord and savior Jesus Christ. I had gotten to a place, where I said to God, Lord Take it away, and I can't do this anymore. He gave me strength, and each time I get weak, he gives me more! I will live to proclaim the glory of the Lord.

To rectify what I had experience in my endeavor. In this endless virtue in my soul, unlimited, infinite, limitless, boundless, continual, perpetual, unfading, interminable, measureless, untold, incalculable, continuous, never-ending, fearless, spirit that lived inside of me. Felt the presence of God around me while standing by myself in the yard I grew up in, in The Island of Jamaica.

Many things of God were overwhelming for me in a sense that God was downloading a lot of spiritual things to show me he wanted to empower me, and use me. I would lose heart as time goes by, would fall out of His plan but would act on my gift, because he had already planted them inside of me.

For you did not receive the spirit of bondage again to fear, but you receive the spirit of adoption by whom we cry "Abba, Father." (Rom. 8:15) The bible says, "All Have sinned and fall short of the glory of God." (Rom 3:23) KJV. We came from wicked and stubborn generation, and once again the bible says, if my people, who are called by my name would humble themselves and pray, and seek my face and change from their wicked ways, then I will hear from heaven, and I will forgive their sins and healed their land. (2Chron. 7:14) KJV seek ye first the kingdom of God and all these things shall be added unto thee (Matt. 6:33) KJV, means you and I to always follow "JESUS" HE is the Lord over our life, amen!

Had this fear of men and what I thought in my mind, "What can men do unto me. Understanding the God that we served, a faithful and wonder working God, He will never leave us nor forsake us, nor our seeds begging bread. (Psalms 37:25) KJV. At one point in my life, my emotions were high, fear tries to step in, but I held on to my Jesus, trusting him and knowing he will carry me through.

Having some encounter knowing God was fighting for me, even the angel would go before me, I could have never been where I am today, if it was not for the Lord Jesus Christ, and for the love of God. There is no fear in love; but perfect love casts out fear, because fear involves torment. Be he who fears has not made perfect in love. (John 4:18) KJV. Thank God for parents who pave the way, set a standard in their homes.

My parents were God fearing individuals, who gave their lives to the Lord, my mother was a humble soul, my dad slipped a few times in front of mine own eyes, fighting with the neighbors and it did concern his children, "never messes with the Williams children". Everyone would know this. He was also a defender for his children's protection, parents are protective of their children, but my dad was extreme. I can speak about the trials and obstacles that endangerment that came my way, we were attacked in many ways more than one.

But the assurance of God sustains us. I can say, "when there is a call on your life, the devil doesn't like you, and many time he will try all that he possible got to kill you and to demolish God's plan for your life. "I would say the devil has some power," but we have the authority of God to trample on scorpions and snakes and be not poison nor to be killed, amen! And over all the power of the enemy. Luke 10:19) KJV, for example, when I decided to come back to the Lord in a personal way, been intimate with God, seeking his face for my children and for my own life, all hell broke loose. I would be leaving my work to an appointment with my hair dresser, and a word of wisdom came to me, my second daughter was in trouble, as I head out to the Salon, I kind of changed my mind, and swung in a whole different direction, heading to my daughter's home where she was living with her husband and her two children at that particular time.

As I enter the home, I notice she was not looking happy, so like her, she tries to hide it from me noticing what was going, "but the spirit of the Lord, already let me receive that knowledge she was in trouble. The husband's other three older children were at the home, they came to visit, and to go swimming in the pool at the Condo. And so I look at her and ask, "What's going on? And as the mom, you know all your children, with my oldest daughter, I would not have to asked, she was verbal, out spoken, whether happy, or sad! And from when I enter her home, she would open up to me. But this daughter of mine would hide it from me. One, she knows, her marriage might have been ended immediately, and she was very easily shamed.

The kids were all ready to go swimming, the husband mention to her while he was taking her kids, "are you coming" but she answers him with an angry tone, no! Looking her in the face, I ask, "why aren't you going," your kids are too young to let them go to the pool, he has his older children, they are going to be playing around in the pool, and won't pay much attention to your smaller ones.

Man, I was itching to go down, then I mention, please let's go. I was hearing what would happen plain as day that she was going to locked up for neglecting her beloved children, and so I had to push for her to see what I saw. We both hurry down to the Lobby of the Condo, they were all playing ball in the water, and the oldest boy had my granddaughter behind him, up against the concrete platform of the pool. Now as we beat on the glass that build across the front of the pool, we realized the child was left by herself, by the boy who had her pinned against the platform with the back of his body.

Literally we were on the outside in the Lobby, yelling for him to acknowledge us, but then he couldn't, the glass was the barrier! I got real radical at that moment, yelled toward the security sitting at his desk, he came immediately and let us in, me seeing the danger, run past my daughter to save the baby girl, who had begun bending over into the water, yes she fell in, but me yelling towards the boy to look behind him, he caught her. God is awesome in is instruction, he takes care of his people, he allowed me to know by the gift of knowledge and discernment the danger that was coming. Which was the work of the Devil. God showed up, angel comes in people form too! For God has not given us a spirit of fear, but of power love and a sound mind. (2Tim. 1:7) had an encounter while my eldest daughter was alive, many, many struggles, she became ill in the 90's was admitted in the hospital, she was sent with a fetes tucked outside of her tube, the doctors never find where it was located in her body.

As she came to stay by my place, she was in excruciating pain, and vomiting until there was nothing left to vomit out of her system, she was constantly looking at me, crying, "mommy help me please" by the time the Government was planning to shut down, The Doctors Hospital in the west end of Toronto, the word of knowledge came again to me, saying for me to call this Hospital, and so I did call and was told to bring her right away, apparently we took a cab to the hospital and she was seen by some Doctors who found where the fetes was, now wouldn't you say, "the devil was a liar" I know that there had to been a way, where it seems to be no way. Faith was what God gives me, even when I didn't know what it was, the mind to listen to God and his angels who fights our battles for us.

Many are called but few are chosen, the bible says, those who are called by my name would humble themselves and pray, and change from their wicked ways. He has called me from I was knitted in my mother's womb. For whatever is born of "GOD" overcomes the world. And this is the victory that has overcome the world---our faith. Faith comes by hearing and by hearing the word of God. (Rom. 10:17) KJV When evil strikes, God shows his people that he owns us, and nothing and no one will ever arm us, some might have a different prospective to this answer, but the bible says, "if you have faith as a mustard seed, you can say moved, to the mountain and it shall be move. (Luke 17:6) KJV Faith pleases God (Heb. 11:6) KJV and He is moved by your faith!

Fear is a stronghold on mankind, it cramps and paralyzed the very core of your being. We as human beings do get fear, even the simplest of the anything, the fear of your child falling off a chair, fear of been hit being hit by a car, fear of your husband been mad at you for spending too much money, even to the fact, you fear of him leaving you, because of your bad spending habits. But the other kind of fear is the fear of the Lord, behold, thus shall the man be blessed who fears the Lord. (Psalms 128:4) KJV The fear of the Lord is: wisdom, knowledge and understanding.

I Had a rigorous vision about my son, about the time every evil forces were exalting themselves against my family and myself, the vision was very clear, there were three men, all dressed in black, came looking for my son, and he had an encounter with them about some individual they killed, and so one of the man popped the question, "did you see anything, now it was obvious to what he saw, then he said, "boy I don't see anything" and they left and didn't hurt him. I was seeing all of this and got up a few days later, talking to my oldest daughter about it, she was in awe of what I was saying. She said mom you are right on the situation that took place. I would say, I am a psalmist in all this, never stop praying for your loved ones, your friends, your relative too and watch what God can do, salvation, healings, faith rises in the ones you share your testimonies with. Sharing the goodness of the Lord Jesus Christ.

 I am a witness to all of this, have faith from an early age, now more faith. The bible speaks of how God gives everyone measure of faith. ((Rom. 12:3) KJV The fear of having children, not knowing who the father was, or where he resided. Now that was a big fear for me, but thank God for the knowledge to take precaution and be mindful of the bad habits and use wisdom in this area. My life revolves around three sets of children. #1 an early pregnancy, so innocent at the time, I thought I could get pregnant on my current situation, (already carrying a child) my God how absurd is that. That happen when you have no experience and don't know what you are doing. #2 is three children from my previous marriage. #3 one from my last relationship. Thank you God for "FAITH" the substance of things hoped for but not yet seen.

A fear of letting the Devil lower me into the hospital to watch a video on amniocentesis, which the Doctor try to hurry me, and convinced me the birth would be defected, because I was just past 30years old, and again wanted me to sign Documents to put a large needle into my stomach, which I refused and walk right of the hospital. Thank you Jesus! Facing the enemy was what I did, taking that leap of faith knowing that God will carry me through the birth of this last baby of mine. She was born after a full course of nine months. Glory to God! (Fear) in my vocabulary is a spirit of fear, the bible says in (Matt. 17:20) KJV if u have faith as a mustard seed, you can say move to that mountain and it shall be moved, meaning the obstacle in your live, with praying and supplication believing it shall be so, God says in Isaiah 43:5 Fear not for I am with thee: I will bring thy seed from the east and gather them from the west.

God tells us do not be afraid, I am your God, in 43: Vs1 But now thus saith the Lord that created thee, Oh Jacob and he that has formed thee, Oh Israel, fear not: for I have redeemed thee, I have called thee by thy name: thou art mine. God wants us to know we are save as long as we choose him. We will have his protection. There was a time in my life that I struggle with a Sheik Witch Doctor who thinks he could destroy me, I was not willing to play the hypocrite, and so I notice some harm that he was sending my way, The psalmist that I am, and with my spiritual eyes made me see right through him. This was my character, "if someone offends me, you bet I am going to see you and let it all out, then we would be fine. No malice was in my heart after I exhale.

God revealed some great revelation for me to acknowledge that he is my protector, my refuge, my savior, my guidance, my joy, my hope, my Jehovah Jireh, my provider, He will supply all your needs according to his riches in glory, by Christ Jesus. My Jehovah Nissi, the Lord is my banner, the name given by mosses to the Altar which he built to celebrate the defeat of the Amalekites at Rephidim.  Victory (Exodus 17:8-17) KJV the Lord will fight our battle, 'JUST TRUST HIM" my Jehovah Rapha my healer. Who heals all my diseases, he will heal you too!
The apostle Paul wrote in Romans 12:6 "If a man's gift is prophesying, let him use it in proportion to his faith" first time you speak out something God has shown you, apparently you are amazed by it, but as you act out in faith while the holy spirit uses you as an oracle of God, it becomes natural, there are times when god tells me something to do, and I don't get it, why?

 Because at the time I might be just thinking that it was my normal fleshly self, thinking it. When later I get the understanding God wanted me to move on what he says for me to do.  At this point in my life, I get it Lord, I am really hearing from you! The time when you stall me from going home, just for me to walk right into someone you order me out of my home to go check the mail, talking to the neighbor, then the real person you wanted to heal, came along, then you let me know by word of knowledge, yes move, and so I start sharing testimonies and the goodness of God. Then Faith rises for this person, I letting them know that God loves them and wants to heal them. During the conversation I popped the question, "are you a born again" standing in the Gap for others is what God as placed upon my heart, with compassion, love, the grace to serve well!

James 2:17 tells us that it is not simply to have faith. We must show faith by what we do. One of the way you can show your faith is to act out in obedience when God directs. Faith without works is dead. (James 2:26) KJV "FAITH THAT DOES NOT SHOW ITSELF BY GOOD WORKS IS NO FAITH AT ALL." So act! But always do so in humility with a desire to serve others. No matter how much of the anointing may be upon you, if you do not use it with a servant heart, then you will get in the way of what God wants to do through you. It is hurting to see someone so puffed up with pride over what God is doing through him, that he actually turns people away from God rather than drawing the lost to His kingdom. But without faith it is impossible to please Him, for he who comes to God must believe that He is, and He is a rewarder of those who diligently seek him. (Heb. 11:6) KJV. That you may walk worthy of the Lord, fully pleasing Him, being fruitful in every good work and increasing in the knowledge of God. (Colossians 1:10)

The truth is all you need is grace: grace that flows from our father's love for us. For it is by grace you have been saved, through faith and this not from yourselves, it is the gift of God-- not by works, so that any man can boast" (Eph. 2:8-9) KJV Ask God to give you a revelation of His grace. When we see the fullness of His grace, we can be completely free from legalism and fear. From the moment you receive Jesus Christ as your Lord and savior, until the day you go home to be with Him, grace is all you need.

- Do not judge by appearance.
- Remember that our battle is against Satan—not people.
- Love everyone including you enemies.
- Weigh your words carefully.
- Love and respect those in authority over you.
- Learn to respect God's timing.
- Love yourself and be happy with the way God made you.

Winnie Smith is a loving mother of five children, lost one daughter in 2012 by an unfortunate situation, and buried her mother close to the same time the following year, 2013. She is a faith leader who believes that God is the great physician, and he is still in the healing business, he also allows the things to happen at His will. Winnie has overcome by the blood of the lamb and by the word of her testimony. "She says, in all things I still trust my God" She is very receptive to the Holy Spirit.  Winnie holds a Certificate in Leadership Public Speaking

- A teacher in Children's Ministry and sings in the Choir at her Church, she is pursuing a BACHELOR OF SYSTEMATIC THEOLOGY @ THE CANADA CHRISTIAN COLLEGE. Looking forward for her Master's Degree Doc. of Divinity at a later time. Winnie believes her apostolic teaching is from the Holy Spirit, holds a Certificate as Lay Evangelist in 2014, she is an Intercessor, also she is officially a prayer partner with The Crossroads Ministries. Winnie has also a prayer line for her Facebook friends to contact: FAITHFULL PRAYER EVANGELIST WINNIE SMITH & looking forward in the future for her own ministry doing the works of the Lord.

- She has mastered some gifts in her early years to Design Clothes and makes them from scratch, took Fashion Designing at George Brown College of Applied Arts & Technology and Seneca College of Applied Arts & Technology. Winnie work's p/t with Matrix Mortgage Global as a Marketing & Sales Consultant. She has a FB PAGE www.facebook.com\divasbridal, Business: House of Diva's Bridal Consultant Mobile, twitter: @houseof_divas, Instagram: HOUSE OF DIVA'S started in 2013 houseofdivasbridal.com will connect you to purchase her new books & products online. Winnie is an Entrepreneur with ability to master any vision she has.

- In 2015 started a line called Fashion Jewellery & Things under the same business; House of Diva's @ events also on FB page. Official online store; fashion-fewelry-and-things.myshopify.com Contact info: 647-381-1508, winniesmith2003@yahoo.ca

# Cami Ferry

**Love is Listening**

The other night, driving home alone after a rather frustrating and emotionally stressful event, I had what I like to think of as one of my very rare, very brief, yet very dramatic emotional breakdowns. I RAILED against God. It's an Irish thing.

"GIVE ME A BREAK!!!", I shouted aloud, "Will You Just Please GIVE ME A BREAK, GOD!! I am doing the best I can!! I am a single mother, a caregiver, a struggling entrepreneur. I am doing the best I can and I am trying to do good for everyone, trying to create Win/Win scenarios and situations for everyone involved. WILL YOU PLEASE JUST GIVE ME SOME HELP!! What More Do YOU Want from ME!?! I am BUSTING MY BUTT here!!" My voice echoed into the solitude that filled the cab of the 1993 Dodge Dakota truck I drive.

Falling into silence and exhaustion, I realized how ridiculous and crazy I must have looked driving along shaking my fist at the sky and I promptly gave thanks that it was late at night and chances are no one saw me. Inside, I felt that familiar emptiness creeping through my veins, ice cold. That feeling of doom that starts as a lump in the pit of my stomach and grows until it engulfs my whole being. Tears welled up in my eyes but I fought them back. I don't like to cry.

Thankfully these times no longer last very long for me and I am now able to shake them off fairly quickly but last year this was not the case. I am not by nature a depressive person. I find it hard not to look on the bright side of things. You could even say that I have always been one of those "Pollyanna Sunshine" type optimists and it has served me well in life especially when I have had those moments of falling into despair and despondency. We all have those moments when we lose HOPE even if only for a short time and 2015 was most definitely one of those times for me.

My second marriage had ended badly in 2013 but I was still living part-time in the same residence as my soon-to-be x-husband in Lodi, California. I was living the other part of the time 127 miles away over the Donner Pass in Sparks, Nevada with my three youngest children and my mom who had fallen at the beginning of the year which resulted in a broken hip, partial hip replacement surgery, and 30 days in a rehab hospital. I had signed her out as her primary caregiver so she could continue to live in her own home but she was no longer able to live alone.

Traveling between the two addresses once, sometimes twice, per week was stressful but necessary in order to care for my three children and my mom as well as build my business down in Lodi, California. It wasn't so much the traveling that caused the deep depression to set in but the stress of that three-hour drive over the pass certainly added to it. The main reason for my bout of depression was the on-going interaction between my x-husband and myself. His ability to increase my self-doubt and decrease my self-worth with his words is uncanny. My logic seeks to inform me that he is emotionally manipulative and that this fact is blatantly clear but there is always that other voice in my head saying, "perhaps not, perhaps he's right, perhaps you are what he says you are, what he has so easily convinced others, even some of your own children, that you are." Of course, I know that I am not what he says I am but sometimes it's very hard to shut those voices of doubt and fear down.

The depression I fell into last year was reminiscent of that which engulfed my life during my first marriage. My first husband was also an abusive, emotionally manipulative, alcoholic man. The difference between the two men I married is 11 years, level of practice at alcohol consumption, and use of physical battery. My first husband was 11 years my senior, a "recovered" alcoholic, and was a wife beater while my second husband is only 9 months older than I, very much a practicing alcoholic, and abusive in every way but physical which is why I often convinced myself during those 25 years that things weren't so bad, after all 'he wasn't hitting me' and 'I had it worse before' right?

Twenty-seven or twenty-eight years prior, I had become so down-trodden, so belittled and beaten by my first husband, that I stood on the roof-top of the flats where I lived down Amelia Street off the Walworth Road in London, England and, looking down at the street below, I seriously contemplated jumping to my death. I was very young but I had lost all hope of a brighter future for myself.

I truly thought that was all there was, that I had what I deserved and there was nothing more for me. I can tell you I spend many nights up on that roof top contemplating an end to my misery but something always stopped me whether it was the thought of the pain it would cause my parents, brother, and loved ones or that glimmer of light at the end of the tunnel, that Pollyanna Sunshine disposition, or perhaps it was the hand of my guardian angel holding me back because he knew that I would come through this and even more to one day discover who I really am and the value of my true worth.

I railed at God in those days, too, angry that I was so oppressed and battered. I stood on that London roof-top shaking my fist at God, crying out in despair for some help, and fighting back those burning tears because I don't like to cry. And again last year, driving back and forth over that treacherous pass, there were many times that I vented my ire at God and His seeming disinterest in the amount of misery that I was suffering through all the while fighting back tears.

Nope, I don't like to cry but sometimes those tears just seem to have a way of streaming down my face, regardless of how hard I resist, and the other night in the cab of the truck after venting my anger at God, that is exactly what they did. The next morning, I still felt basically hopeless, all my work, all my efforts seemed to have been for nothing and it seemed that, once again, God hadn't been listening.

Then as if to prove me wrong, I received a call out-of-the-blue from someone who offered me some help. How can I explain the timing of this call other than to say it was in God's time? I have come so far in building a bright and "Pollyanna Sunshine" future for myself, my children, and my mom. I now live with four of my six children and my mom in a house in Lodi. I no longer have to deal with the emotional manipulation and verbal abuse. I AM FREE!! I have peace. I can stand in my own power and hold my head high for I am no longer a willing victim. I am a committed, focused, worthy, and abundant woman!

But there are times like the other night where it just seems like all my hard work and effort is amounting to nothing and then those voices come back into my head with their mantra of self-doubt, negativity, and fear. There are still times when I wonder if God even cares but then He surprises me with evidence that SOMEONE is Listening.

He sends me a call from someone who has a solution and who is willing to help. That call was like a lifeline being thrown out to me as I was drowning in despair and desolation. That call was a GOD SEND, an Angel, Proof that SOMEONE was Listening!! As I took that call while I was running errands with my eldest daughter, I expressed to the caller how divine her timing was and how I had just been expressing my increasing despair to my daughter in the very moment that my phone rang.

We are not abandon. We are precious and loved beyond imagination. Regardless of how it sometimes feels, God is a God of Love and He hears the cry of the poor! Praise Be to God!!

As I write this, the tears are streaming down my cheeks but I'm not resisting this time because these are tears of joy not tears of fear!

**"Love recognizes no barriers. It jumps hurdles, leaps fences, penetrates walls to arrive at its destination full of hope."**
       ~ Maya Angelou


Cami Ferry - Founder/Artistic Director of In Motion Theatre Company, Founder of Cami's Cardio, Co-Host and Partner of Rush Hour for Success Radio show on Money 105.5FM Thursdays and Fridays at 2pm PST, and executive team member of the Solutions4Life program.

Cami is an actress, singer, and dancer with 30 years of professional training and experience in classical theatre, opera & voice, as well as ballet, jazz, and contemporary dance in London, England and the U.S. Through her company, In Motion Theatre, she has co-produced and starred in award winning Independent films.

She is an author having written several articles for various publications. She is currently completing her certification as a Health and Fitness Coach as well as preparing to enter into the competitive/professional realm of Latin and Ballroom Dance. She has also recently entered into the Financial Arena with Exertus Financial Partners and will be obtaining her license.

Cami is the mother of six wonderful children, three boys/three girls, and Grandma to her Grandbabies, Nathan (1yr) & Cassy (age 1 month). Cami is also very blessed to be the caregiver to her mom who has positively influenced her life in many ways and is her biggest fan.

Cami Ferry
2133 W. Pine Street, Lodi, CA 95242
209-663-9953
cferry@InMotionTheatre.org
www.InMotionTheatre.org
https://www.facebook.com/cami.e.ferry
https://www.facebook.com/InMotionTheatreCompany/
https://www.facebook.com/rushhourforsuccess/

# Dr Dikabo Mogopodi

**Life is not on my clock, embracing the pain of the wait**

It was a good thing I never choose the front pews in church. I ran outside almost hitting the door, escaping the stares of the congregation. I didn't want people to start wondering why a girl would break into tears at another girl's wedding. I didn't want the nosey sisters speculating that may be the groom broke my heart. Just outside the church compound, I found a tree where I moved a rock towards the shades and sat there. I looked at how dry the tree was, with leaves drying and falling off, ironically reminding me how strength was withering from my soul. I sobbed out of control.

My head throbs. I dial my sister's number Ndira. She has always been my go to person when I feel broken. I have six sisters. Each sister serves a different function. One I would call for prayers, one to gloat about any little achievement because she is always intrigued by the events of my life, to others I am a pillar of strength despite me being the youngest. But Ndira, God bless her, is for the broken heart, she knows how to mend it. She tries to calm me with no success. So she asks me to text her details of my whereabouts. We text each other back and forth. What was she to do when we were over 300 kilometers apart? I didn't know she would send someone to find me.

A few minutes later Fingi, a friend who over the years has earned her place as more of a sister than a friend finds me. It is Ndira who has sent her.

"You are going to be fine" that is all she says and the rest of the time she holds me. I feel better, this is God reaching to me through the human touch. I don't go back to the ceremony I drive back home. May it was going to be a while before I find healing. This was the first wedding I had attended after my father's wedding may be that is why I responded the way I did. No one should lose their father before their wedding. It was the moment Amo, the bride, had tendered her hand to her father and smiled that I was reminded what my father would miss. Amazing how someone's moment of joy can awaken another's heartache.

It had been my father's wish as much as mine to walk me down the aisle. We had picked a song we would walk to. It wasn't going to be here comes the bride. No. Ours was going to be a hymn that would represent what me and my father believe of life;

> ***Honour and glory be given to God of Light***
>
> ***The Lord God who created us***
>
> ***His works shine forever illuminating the earth***
>
> ***Let Honour and glory be given to him***
>
> ***Till the end of seasons***
>
> ***Praise be to God at all seasons,***
>
> ***Honour belongs to him.***
>
> ***Honour belongs to him"***

My father had always spoken for education, encouraging me to put my very best and when I attained my PhD in my 20s it was his proudest moment. But somehow he had always maintained that it all was God's doing. So him and I were both of the understanding that all I had become was because of God and he deserved that honour. My heart had hang onto the moment we would walk together like a treasure.

I had been hopeful that he would make it despite the signs of deteriorating health, until the dreadful call from my mother. "You have to come home." She had said, "It would be better if you see your father". Only a month before my wedding. How could this be? The next morning, I had jumped into the earliest bus. Three hours had seemed like five years. I kept checking the phone clock every minute. Serowe had never been so far. As soon as the bus arrived I jumped off at Sekgoma Memorial hospital. My father looked frail with all types of tubes and drips all over his body. I had greeted him and he had tried to say something. 'He can't talk' my mother had said. I had broken into tears and walked out. I could not bear the sight of pain. Yes it was the type of pain you could almost see touch and smell and it was too much to handle.

Me, my sisters and their spouses had pleaded with God, begging him to spare the man who had been central to our lives. We held hands as we proclaimed the Lord's healing. I had said to God "if u save him for just two more months or at least just enough time for my wedding I won't ask for anything else after this". I lied. But this is what desperation does. My sister Kux, the one I go to for prayers had called every pastor she knows.

This was war and she was willing to say her last prayers if she had to. For almost a week we had pastors joining us for prayers and people all over praying with us over the phone. We had surrounded my father with love every other day at the hospital, refusing to let him die but no amount of praying could keep him alive.

We lost him to battle of illness that had started as ulcers and eventually cancer. I was never one to question God, to say why me, because I had been taught that he always has a reason. But the death of my father a month before my wedding had not left me unscathed. Couldn't God just spare him for an extra month? A part of me felt guilty though, guilty that perhaps I wasn't thankful enough, that mine was a lighter pain, that other kids never had a single chance with their fathers. I felt guilty that perhaps I was not entitled to grieving. May be I was bordering on selfishness. How can I want a life to be spared on my account just so I can make a 5-minute walk? Was I even entitled to life extension? I had debated with myself.

Five months later after, March 7 2009, that girl who ran away from Amo's wedding walks down the aisle and at the end stands a man she would say I do to. The girl is wearing a spotless ball gown white wedding dress. And that girl is me. The song played as I would have it. Here was a beautiful Saturday morning. As I take the walk I know I am not just going to be fine, I am fine.

I feel joy and peace. It isn't my father I walk with but it is my Uncle Ramothwa who has the heart of the father, he has filled every gap that needed to be filled. And he is not the only one, Uncle Bas has done the same and many other people. They have reached deep into their pockets and deep into their hearts. They have given everything that they could give. I have found comfort and peace through people God brought into my life. I know I will miss my dad but I have found strength.

"I thought you were gonna cry". My new husband said as he hugged me "you were very brave." I let my head rest on his chest resisting the urge to cry. Maybe I was very brave, maybe I wasn't, maybe I just learnt a new way of trusting God, that trust is not always about expectation but it is about leaning on God and his people, the ones he plants on our paths. There were people that had been planted on my path, at work, at church, friends who encouraged me to snap out of grief. 'We have to set the new wedding date soon. Remember your dad had built his own marriage and I am sure he would have wanted you to build yours' Goitse, one of my friends, had said.

I had also been given the understanding of what it means that all things work together for the good to those who love God. I still miss my father. I have missed him during monumental times like the time when my kids were born. I have missed the long educational conversations which were always full of substance. But life does not happen on my clock nor anybody's clock and it will continue to take directions we didn't plan for. When it does we must yield it all to God, our brokenness our doubts and our anger.

Through my loss I have become stronger and I now know that life does not work on my clock, I know that just because we want something does not mean we will have it on our time. I also know now that in that our truly heartbreaking moments God will not withhold his love for us. He will make the painful moments beautiful and that is what grace is about, God reaching out to us and reminding us that our painful moments aren't trash because that is where we find him and we find friends.

Life still surprises me; it throws punches that I didn't see coming. But I have learnt that sometimes I ought not to try to punch back or even push back the pain and perhaps throw it some place I should never remember. I have learnt that sometimes I should surrender and let life happen on God's clock.

So what if the things you pray for something and you never receive? What if life messes up your schedules, your clocks and rearrange your plans? Because that is what life will do. Dreams will get delayed some will get broken. Perhaps the real freedom is in knowing that God will show up for us. That God's got this.

Our clocks, our times shouldn't be all what matters. The real freedom comes in knowing that we can't want to escape the pain, we shouldn't have to fear it. Because just may be the pain is not meant to be escaped, nor feared but it is meant to be embraced, may be life is not meant to be controlled but to be lived. And that is what I am still learning to embrace and live and find grace that hides behind the pain.

Dr Dikabo Mogopodi is a wife to Samuel Raditloko, a fabulous mother of 2 boys. She loves God and is passionate about cooking and writing. She is from Botswana, Africa. She is an inspirational blogger at www.sunrisemoment.com. In her teens she wrote a book entitled "Is there hope in the wilderness?" which was published after much struggle in her 20s. She holds a PhD in analytical chemistry which was a sandwich between University of Botswana and University of Oslo. She works as a researcher and has published some of her scientific work in scientific journals of high impact. She speaks for education and holds talks in schools to inspire learning and inspire a girl child to take up science courses. She also speaks at churches and in different organizations to inspire young people. She contributes to other blogs, she loves travelling. She believes in the possibilities of dreams and that Africa too has a place in the international platform. Twitter handle @lovingmysunrise, https://www.facebook.com/Sunrisemoment4U

# Charmella Y. Smith

#FearIsBehindMe

*Romans 8:21*
*that the creation itself will be set free from its bondage to corruption and obtain the freedom of the glory of the children of God*

It all started to come to fruition when I made a conscious decision that I would make a public declaration that I was putting **FEAR** Behind me literally; at a tattoo party I decided to follow through and make my declaration permanent and branded on the skin of my being. Having #Fear tattooed on the back just under my neck. I was now conveying the message indefinitely no more impactful than my feelings, emotions or thoughts; this will never go away and I need to LIVE as if Fear is behind me.

Prior to the tattoo party, I had fell into depression as my last two children were emerging into adulthood. The hamster wheel of survival that I had been on, my day to day, month to month, year to year reality would be coming to a complete halt. I would need to deal with the wounds I had buried; I would really have to Face my Fear!

Once I decided to release myself from concealing the sexual abuse that I suffered, I began to initiate internal healing and that's when I began to start the journey to be FREE, until that time I was living in Fear.

Freedom is a choice. It is not an automatic right. Freedom has a hefty cost. Freedom doesn't come by chance.

There was more damage to my future. The more I held onto the past. My continued failed relationships romantic and platonic were because of my unintentional fear of my truth that needed to be shared!

I needed to consciously make a choice to face the scariest of all things for my greater good, not just for me but for the imparting to others in very similar situations who looked just like me, made up. Great pretenders and master façade orchestrator not all but some. I lived with shame, guilt and deep rooted relationship issues dealing with trust and betrayal. I was in prison of my potential coming...

I was living a lie and my freedom was in my truth that needed to be released; through courage and desire. I wanted to lift the weight of the lies. I had told myself for a long time or just about ALL of my adult life.

It was not easy to open up the box of suppressed emotions and pain of the secrets inappropriate sexual encounters. A child whose innocence was stripped away through various acts with young men double my age at the time.

I buried that little girl down inside of my Executive persona, that I fought to be for the next 20+ years. I could accomplish anything I set my mind to do, being in control of accomplishments was easy, looking fine and behaving somewhat fine was easy. I only recognized her in times of complete solitude and isolation triggered by great disappointment of betrayal, abandonment or rejection.

Yet the cost has calculated beyond my natural abilities to level the playing field; I need to Pay back this debt.
I owe it to her to settle this; the reward is far too great. What was on the other side of Fear? To reveal my truth was more intriguing for the possibility of a New reality. A level of Freedom that you can't buy!

Now is the time to take a chance to relinquish the pain and face the distress for a better sense of life. To release myself from the acts of destruction to be blameless. And to know that I have value in spite of the act that stole life from me for many years.

The ability to accept someone that hurt me as a person who needs to be forgiven, to be considered for their inabilities and weakness. To Forgive became a strong desire, yet every time I tried; something happened to me. Something that would continue to silence my truth and keep me bound in internal pain, stagnant and numbness to the colors of life. Everything seemed grayscale. I wanted the colors of life.

## " The Soul becomes dyed with the color of its thoughts." Marcus Aurelius

Choosing Forgiveness gave me a glimpse of color. I saw the color Yellow, it was easy it was soft, gentle and it was safe. Though my desire for freedom was an illustration of a beautiful portrait surrounding Love, which visually was red which was a warning color but also power and authority the feeling Forgiveness gave me. Through Faith I saw Pink, to believe it's possible to be FREE from the weight of the lies. I couldn't release the deception. I needed to Believe in my Heart that I could be Free.

**The only way to have the ultimate level of FREEDOM is to face FEAR!**

Fear always represents Black. It's dark and sometimes never ending. If you allow it to be; adding a glimpse of light into the darkness can change the color and develop the outcome.

I mean look it square in the face and refuse to return to the isolation, or remain a prisoner of it...

Often times the thing that has you captive is the very thing that will catapult you to the most amazing life experience you are destined to have! You just have to have faith and believe.

Take courage in identifying FEAR in your life and start conquering your NEXT!

For me it was dealing with Domestic Violence of Sexual, Emotional and Physical Abuse that had plagued my life. And I was able to Face My FEAR, dig deep into the pain and pull out my purpose!

I know that may sound cliché but I promise it's that simple! True Freedom comes from challenging our comfort level and self-analysis.

All acts of Fear have a significant purpose to our next level in our lives. For me it was recognizing the signs in the youth, I mentored as a foster care advocate. My ability to help them face their lies of deception and release the weight to walk in Freedom.

Today I challenge you to Face your fears by writing down 7 Fears that are holding you back from Ultimate Freedom.

To be aware is the most important step to Freedom!
It may be painful to do so, give yourself time and put a strategy together to deal with these one by one.
Here are 7 ways for you to work from FEAR to Freedom.
You must understand and identify that Fear will never disappear!

**So our objective is to**
- Face Fear by acknowledging what Fear is in your life
- Examine Fear and locate its origin
- Choose Faith the opposite of Fear and the game changer to manage Fear
- Measure your strategic plan to beat FEAR and what you need to adjust to Gain your FREEDOM
- Preparation beats Failure and builds confidence necessary to win
- Move with Fear, go in spite of the Fears illusion your plan and preparation will eradicate ALL Fear
- Conquer Fear and live in Freedom

**Now be prepared to experience a new level of living, Welcome to Freedom, No Fear!**

**"Put Fear in its place; BEHIND you, DO it Afraid if necessary and Don't look back, Welcome to Freedom!"**

Charmella Y. Smith is an Author, Real Estate Expert and Youth advocate. She is also an educator, teaching classes to first time Home Buyers to establish sustainable communities in Central Ohio. As a service oriented professional and youth advocate, Charmella cares deeply about issues impacting young women.

She was a Teenage mother whom is a survivor of physical and sexual abuse who identifies her affiliation with Franklin County Children Services as an emancipated youth at 17.

Charmella is determined to exhort, ignite, and inspire; Her experience working with young women with no foolproof plan for interdependence inspired her to establish a nonprofit foundation called Women of Sovereignty.

It supports young women who are aging out/aged out of foster care, helping them to Prevent homelessness. The foundation teaches Financial literacy as a catalyst to Self Sufficiency; WOS provides safety skills to combat Human trafficking, to Improve Self Esteem and Emotional support to become a Positive Influence of society.

The Foundation host its annual community walk for Domestic Violence Awareness Month in October in collaboration with National Domestic Violence Awareness Month.

Charmella has received an International women's day award for Education, Who's Who in Black Columbus and a Community spotlight among her fellow Realtors as well as the Million dollar sales award and the list goes on.

For Speaking or info visit her website at

www.charmellayvonne.in

# Christine DiDio

**Surrender to Serenity**
**My journey of self-discovery and soulful healing**

It was a day like any other, where I was sitting at my computer and reading my emails. Unknowingly, this day was going to alter the rest of my life. As I looked at the email left open on the monitor for all to see, my heart felt as if it had been encased in glass and shattered to millions of pieces. It was our family computer we shared and typically my children did their school work on. Fortunately, on that particular day, I was the first one to notice the email with a person's name I did not recognize.

My daughter was getting ready to graduate from high school in 2009 and I was thrilled she was accepted to the University of Santa Barbara. My parents, my brother and my in-laws were coming to California to help celebrate. It was a happy occasion for us all, and we were excited to have our family here during this special day.

After reading the email, my first thought was there must be some type of mistake. Unfortunately, that was not to be the case. It's amazing to me that only a few paragraphs, could shatter my world and my heart in the blink of an eye. The man I was married to for almost twenty years, who I had committed to love and honor to death do us part, now seemed like the lowest form of life. I reread the email again and again just to make sure it was real and that it was not just a dream. Staring with shock, disbelief and anger, was another woman declaring her undying love for my husband. I can only describe the pain I felt like a dagger pierced through my heart and torn in half.

I loved my spouse, sure we had our ups and downs like any other married couple but I never suspected that he was capable of such a betrayal. In my darkest moment of anger, despair and heartache, my initial thought was to give up on almost twenty years of marriage. However, I was incredibly torn between staying for my children's sake and leaving to preserve my own happiness.

My children were both teenagers at the time and although they were older, had to deal with their own burdens of grief and anger. I did the best I could to maintain the routine and not add any additional stress to their lives. However, some days we were all so sad and upset it was easier to lock ourselves away from the world. For years, I had been the peacemaker, problem solver and the glue which held our family together. In my weakened state, I did not think I had the ability to stay strong emotionally, especially for my children's sake.

In 2008, I needed to have foot surgery. Back then I do not know which pain was worse, the physical pain of my surgery or the pain of my shattered heart? If I had to choose one, I would say emotional pain is far worse than the physical pain. However, it was through the healing of my physical body which gave me the strength and determination to move forward with the divorce.

My former spouse used to tell me my expectations were too high. Looking back, I realize he was right. I do have certain expectations which include; faithfulness, love, honor and commitment from someone. I should not be made to feel guilty for wanting a man to meet these requirements. If I stayed I would be sending a message to my children that it

was ok to settle with someone who did not love me or value my worth. Although I could forgive him, I knew in my heart I could not trust him again. Fortunately, I was very blessed to have a strong support system from my family and friends. Even though my parents lived thousands of miles away, they were always there for me when I needed them.
At the time, I was attending a Christian church and I remember asking God; "why did this have to happen?" It was during these dark moments of devastation, which I turned away from God instead of towards him; when I needed him most. I was hurt beyond belief and had so much anger and resentment which I needed to let go of in order to heal. I eventually realized that God was not to blame for this and I am glad I found out the truth. With the help of my pastor and friends, I returned back to my faith.

During our separation, I was working as a Behavioral Therapist, helping children diagnosed with autism. My main concern was how could I help a child in need when I was having difficulty staying strong. I had considered moving back to Massachusetts, but since my funds were limited and my son wanted to finish his last few years of high school in California, I decided to stay and look for a home to rent.
I felt guilty that I did something wrong which caused him to search for someone else.

However, in my moment of truth, I knew I needed to love myself more and not settle for less than my worth. Once I gave up control over my situation, I left it in God's hands to help guide me and knew in my heart it was time to let him go. I also realized it was not my responsibility to try to change him, but to work through my own insecurities and fears and learn to change myself.

Ultimately, I came to the decision that I loved him enough to give him his freedom and let him go while also choosing to love myself more by having the courage to walk away. Looking back, I admit this was the most difficult decision I ever made, but once made there was no turning back.

In 2010, I placed my house up for a short sale and began the journey of looking for something more economical. I had the opportunity for a fresh start and I was blessed to have kind and caring friends who helped me pack and move out of my house. During that time, my daughter had just graduated from high school and was accepted at UCSB. I was not sure how I was going to afford to send her to college, but she was so determined; I knew she would find a way to not give up on her dream.

My son took the separation much harder than I anticipated. His grades began to drop and he isolated himself away from his friends and family. In 2011, he was badly burned in a backyard fire pit while staying at a friend's house. To see any child injured is heartbreaking, but to see your own child suffering is an awful pain because it leaves you feeling helpless. It was also a painful reminder to me regarding the fact I was alone and no longer had the emotional support from my spouse. I helped wrap my son's wounds for weeks and researched every possible remedy to help his burns heal faster. The burn center thought he would have severe scarring but fortunately, he was blessed with a miraculous healing and minimal scarring. I wish he did not have to go through so much pain, but he was so brave through his entire healing process and seldom complained. There is no greater love than a mother's love and if I could, would have traded places with him than to see him suffer. This was when I made the conscious decision to find God again. I was shown miracles exist every day; I was just too blind to see them at the time.

Several years later he fractured his back and it was through his physical therapy that he decided to declare a new college major of Kinesiology. I do believe everything happens for a reason, but at the time of trials, it is sometimes difficult to determine the right path to take. My son continues to work full time and attend college. While my children and I are not the same people we used to be, through our trials of perseverance, each of us have become better at accepting the things in life which are beyond our control.

During this time period, I was faced with the decision of what am I going to do for the rest of my life? In 2011, I was given the wonderful opportunity to train for a life and health insurance agent. It was the day of my first interview and I had hives, the size of quarters on my face. I did not want to go on the interview for fear of humiliation. Fortunately, my interviewer was sympathetic to my plight. The Dermatologist I went to initially diagnosed me with lupus, but afterward, my lab work revealed it was an allergic reaction to a food product and stress induced.

During this dark period, my life seemed to be spiraling out of control with every fear imaginable. I had lost close to twenty pounds as a result of my separation and could not seem to find closure or inner healing. A close friend of mine convinced me to talk to a priest which was the best advice I had received. After speaking to our church pastor, he convinced me to return to church. I began to notice a difference in my life in a short amount of time. I felt like I was being reborn and it was the initial phase of healing my heart from what once had felt like shattered glass. For years, I carried around my emotional baggage which I knew I needed to let go of my past. The first step of my healing process was to forgive my ex completely. My self-esteem was in need of repair and unconsciously I was attracting the exact relationships I knew I did not want. This defense mechanism was the only way I felt I could protect my heart by not allowing myself to receive the love I knew I was worthy of. However, my fear of being alone was far more terrifying than being in the wrong relationship.

In 2011, I received my California Health and Life Insurance license. At the time, I did not see myself as an insurance salesperson but I knew I could help people protect their health and finances and was excited to begin a new career. After a year of selling life insurance at my first company, I realized their values did not match my own and I needed to find a new insurance company. My prayers were answered when a new opportunity came two days later after a friend referred me to someone looking for a new life and health agent. One door closed and another door opened as my current employer became a great mentor and friend and still continues to provide encouragement.

After enrolling health clients, it seemed shortly after signing each person up for health care needed hospital care for cancer treatments, pneumonia, heart surgery or broken bones. I am not a believer in coincidence and knew that God was providing intervention. I was grateful to help so many people and was rewarded by their expressed gratitude. The client who needed heart surgery called me his life saver. His doctor said he was very fortunate he attained health insurance when he did because it saved his life. Although the glory did not belong to me, it was an amazing feeling to be able to help so many people.

I continued to educate myself and relied on my faith and intuition to guide me towards becoming a Relationship Life Coach. This training not only helped me to see the beauty of motivating and inspiring others, it helped me to discover who I truly was. I also joined several nonprofit groups which support community members and high school students in the fight against bullying. The more people I helped, the more my soul began to feel a sense of calmness

During my divorce, I experienced emotions of grief and loss and needed to release my anger, which was a necessary part of my healing process. It was through forgiveness and acceptance, I finally was able to let go of all my anger and began to have renewed purpose and hope. Eventually, I began to feel at peace with myself and felt like the weight of the world was being lifted off my shoulders. I learned to be happy being me and rediscovering my childhood passions of writing and painting. I now define my success by the many people I am able to help as a Health Agent and as a Life Coach.

Through my perseverance of never giving up hope, God's guidance and following my heart and intuition; I have regained my confidence and independence. I began to put my complete trust and faith in God's hands and to learn to accept people for who they are. I also learned a difficult life lesson of letting go of negative people in my life, sadly, even though it meant I still cared about them.

My journey continues based on faith, trust, love, peace and compassion and most importantly, forgiveness. Although I cannot change my past hurts, I certainly have a new outlook on life. I am grateful for the mistakes I made along the way, as well as the wonderful soulful friends I met on my journey of self-discovery. It was through the ability to forgive and truly let go of my fears, which helped me to release my emotional blocks and break the chains that bind. With my trust placed in God's hands, I know he had a better plan for my future than I could ever have imagined.

Every choice made on my soul journey has brought me to where I am today. I have returned to a state of peace through forgiveness, renewal, letting go, love and healing through faith and surrender. I am grateful for the opportunity to share my story with others; and that it provide a message of inspiration, encouragement, and hope. Had I not chosen to surrender to God's will, I would not have realized my mission in life, helping others attain peace within their soul.

Christine DiDio is a licensed CA Health & Life Specialist and Relationship Life Coach; who can guide you in all areas of your life; from learning to love yourself and teaching you to let go of negative emotions. With a distinctive style of empathy and intuitiveness; her mission is to help others through the pains of divorce and suffering. She seeks to provide women with a message of hope, encouragement and healing.

Born and raised in Andover, Massachusetts and Rome, Italy; she now resides in California with her two grown children. Her passions include exercising, journaling, trips to the beach and spending time with family and friends.

She graduated from Northern Essex Community College and Bentley University with a degree in Business Management. In 2011, she became a licensed CA Health and Life Agent and in 2015 became a Certified Life Coach in order to offer her clients an added quality of customer service.
Currently offering new clients their first 30 minutes of free coaching.

**"Helping others to bare their heart and soul"**
peace2thesoul@gmail.com
www.peace2thesoul.com
(209) 629-2380

# Conclusion

This amazing anthology is filled with beautiful and inspiring stories. From all parts of the world. Each uniquely written and shared by these inspirational authors.

I am so blessed to be the complier and had the honor of helping each woman share her testimony! God is always good! He has an amazing way of turning our troubles into his triumphs!

I hope each of you who read this book are touched and inspired by these stories. Take a moment to remember there are no coincidences! God is always in control! Always has you in the palm of his hand.

If you let him he will use and take you places you never dreamed of. We started this book with a prayer and I will end it with one too.

**Dear Heavenly Father:**

**Please bless each reader and each author of this book. May they find and take exactly what you have for them. May they use it to follow you and change the world. May they be blessed and learn to be a blessing to others. May they learn to love, forgive, have faith and always trust in your plan. May they learn to collaborate and not compete. And to work together to further your Kingdom.**

**Amen.**

Made in the USA
Middletown, DE
17 March 2017